HAR___ -
DAVIDSON
WLA MANUAL
1944

HARLEY-DAVIDSON
WLA MANUAL
1944

US WAR DEPARTMENT

AMBERLEY

First published in 1944
This edition published 2014

Amberley Publishing
The Hill, Stroud
Gloucestershire, GL5 4EP

www.amberley-books.com

British Library Cataloguing in Publication Data.
A catalogue record for this book is available from the British Library.

ISBN 978 1 4456 4341 0 (print)
ISBN 978 1 4456 4349 6 (ebook)

Typesetting and Origination by Amberley Publishing.
Printed in the UK.

Contents

Introduction

The Harley-Davidson WLA was produced to US Army specifications during and around the Second World War. It was an adaptation of an existing civilian model, the WL, the 45 solo type, having a 45-cubic-inch (740 cm3) engine displacement and single-rider design. Harley-Davidson began producing the WLA in 1940, as part of it's expanding military division. The entry of the United States into the Second World War saw over 90,000 being produced during the war (along with spare parts etc). Harley-Davidson would also produce a close WLA variant for the Canadian Army called the WLC and would supply small numbers to the UK, South Africa, and others.

Interestingly, all of the WLAs made after the attack on Pearl Harbor, regardless of when they were constructed, would be given serial numbers showing 1942 production. Therefore, war-time machines would come to be known as 42WLAs. This may have been in recognition of the continued use of the same specification.

Many WLAs would be shipped under the Lend-Lease program. The largest recipient was the Soviet Union, who bought over 30,000 WLAs. Production of the WLA ceased after the war, but grew again during the Korean War.

Most WLAs after the war were sold and 'civilianised'. The many motorcycles available at very low cost led directly to the

rise of the chopper and other modified motorcycle styles, as well as the surrounding biker culture. Many a young soldier would come home hoping to get the same Harley-Davidson he rode in the service, leading to the post-war popularity of both the motorcycle and the company in general.

However, this also ensured that few original WLAs survived in the US and Europe. A few of WLAs were left in the Soviet Union, and either stored or put in private hands. With little access to parts and no chopper culture, and no export path to the West, many of those motorcycles were actually preserved during the years of the Cold War. Russia and other former Soviet countries are now a major source of WLAs and parts.

The WLA is, as mentioned, very similar to the WL. There are, however, several specific changes that make it a military model:

The paint and other finishes: paint was usually olive or black and chrome and nickel-plated parts were blued or painted white. Some were left as plain aluminum.

Blackout lights: to reduce visibility WLAs were fitted with a second set of blackout head and tail lights.

Fenders: to reduce mud clogging, the sides of the normal fenders were removed.

Accessories: a luggage rack for radio equipment was included, along with an ammo box, leather Thompson submachine gun holster, skid plate, leg protectors, and a windshield could be fitted.

Air cleaner: an oil bath air cleaner, used in many cases for tractors and other vehicles in dusty environments, was fitted

to handle the detritus of off-road use and to allow easier field maintenance.

Fording: changes to the crankcase breather made it less likely that there would be water intake into the crankcase.

In 1944, the US War Department published this manual for troops ahead of entering the Second World War. In addition to a basic description of the motorcycle, and how to ride it, this manual contained all the technical information required for identification, use and care of the materiel. It is the essential guide for any owner, giving vehicle maintenance instructions for many technical issues, and no doubt saved many soldiers' lives out in the field.

PART ONE—OPERATING INSTRUCTIONS

Section I

INTRODUCTION

1. SCOPE.

a. This technical manual* is published for the information and guidance of the using arm personnel charged with the operation, maintenance, and minor repair of this materiel.

b. In addition to a description of the Harley-Davidson motorcycle, this manual contains technical information required for the identification, use, and care of the materiel. The manual is divided into two parts. Part One, section I through section VI, gives vehicle operating instructions. Part Two, section VII through section XXV, gives vehicle maintenance instructions to using arm personnel charged with the responsibility of doing maintenance work within their jurisdiction.

c. In all cases where the nature of the repair, modifications, or adjustment is beyond the scope or facilities of the unit, the responsible ordnance service should be informed so that trained personnel with suitable tools and equipment may be provided, or proper instructions issued.

2. SUPERSESSION OF QUARTERMASTER MANUALS.

a. This technical manual, together with TM 9-1879, supersedes and replaces the following Quartermaster Corps publications:

(1) TM 10-1175—Maintenance manual, motorcycle, solo, Harley-Davidson (Model 42-WLA), 11 September 1941.

(2) TM 10-1177—Maintenance manual, motorcycle, solo, Harley-Davidson (Models 1940-41-42), 11 September 1941.

(3) TM 10-1331—Maintenance manual, motorcycle, chain drive Harley-Davidson (Model 42 WLA, solo).

(4) TM 10-1359—Instruction folder (45-A) motorcycles, solo, Harley-Davidson (Model 1941 WLA 45), 25 November 1941.

(5) TM 10-1361—Instruction folder (45-B) motorcycle, solo, Harley-Davidson (Model 1941 WLA 45), 25 November 1941.

---

*To provide operating instructions with the materiel, this technical manual has been published in advance of complete technical review. Any errors or omissions will be corrected by changes or, if extensive, by an early revision.

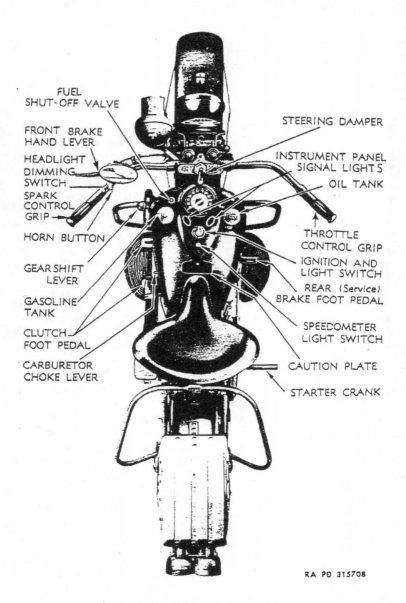

FUEL
SHUT-OFF VALVE

FRONT BRAKE
HAND LEVER

HEADLIGHT
DIMMING
SWITCH

SPARK
CONTROL
GRIP

HORN BUTTON

GEAR SHIFT
LEVER

GASOLINE
TANK

CLUTCH
FOOT PEDAL

CARBURETOR
CHOKE LEVER

STEERING DAMPER

INSTRUMENT PANEL
SIGNAL LIGHTS

OIL TANK

THROTTLE
CONTROL GRIP

IGNITION AND
LIGHT SWITCH

REAR (Service)
BRAKE FOOT PEDAL

SPEEDOMETER
LIGHT SWITCH

CAUTION PLATE

STARTER CRANK

RA PD 315708

Figure 1—Top View of Motorcycle

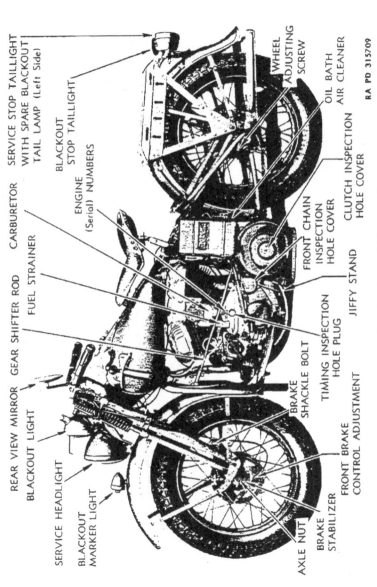

REAR VIEW MIRROR   GEAR SHIFTER ROD   CARBURETOR

BLACKOUT LIGHT   FUEL STRAINER

ENGINE (Serial) NUMBERS

SERVICE STOP TAILLIGHT WITH SPARE BLACKOUT TAIL LAMP (Left Side)

BLACKOUT STOP TAILLIGHT

WHEEL ADJUSTING SCREW

OIL BATH AIR CLEANER

RA PD 315709

SERVICE HEADLIGHT

BLACKOUT MARKER LIGHT

AXLE NUT

BRAKE STABILIZER

FRONT BRAKE CONTROL ADJUSTMENT

BRAKE SHACKLE BOLT

TIMING INSPECTION HOLE PLUG

JIFFY STAND

FRONT CHAIN INSPECTION HOLE COVER

CLUTCH INSPECTION HOLE COVER

Figure 2—Left Side View of Motorcycle

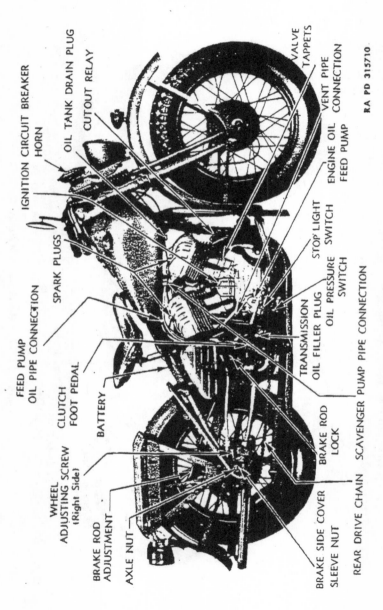

Figure 3—Right Side View of Motorcycle

DESCRIPTION AND TABULATED DATA

3. DESCRIPTION (figs. 1, 2, and 3).

a. This 2-cylinder solo motorcycle is powered by a V-type, air-cooled gasoline engine, operating on conventional 4-stroke, 4-cycle principles. Air-cooled engines rely upon movement of air over cylinder and head radiating fins, and upon circulation of oil for dissipation of excessive heat. Motorcycle engines, therefore, under no conditions should be operated for more than 1 minute when motorcycle is not in motion.

4. DATA.

a. Vehicle Specifications.

Type of engine .... 2-cylinder, V-type L-head, air-cooled

Cylinder bore .... $2\frac{3}{4}$ in.

Stroke .... $3\frac{13}{16}$ in.

Engine number (serial) left side engine base, below front cylinder.

Wheelbase .... 4 ft $11\frac{1}{2}$ in.

Length over-all .... 7 ft 4 in.

Width over-all (handle bars) .... 3 ft 5 in.

Wheel size .... 18 in.

Tire size .... 4.00 x 18 in.

Tire type .... Drop center

Weight of vehicle (without rider or armament) .... 540 lb

Ground clearance (skid plate) .... 4 in.

Kind and grade of fuel .... Gasoline: 72 octane or higher

High gear ratio 4.59:1

Engine sprocket 31-tooth

Countershaft sprocket 17-tooth

Rear wheel sprocket 41-tooth

b. Performance.

Maximum allowable speed .... 65 mph

Miles per gallon (hard surface) 35

Cruising range (without refill)......................100 miles

Fording depth (carburetor) ....18 in.

c. Capacities.

Fuel capacity (left tank)........................3⅜ U.S. gal

Oil tank capacity (right tank)...................1⅛ U.S. gal

Transmission capacity ....¾ pt

Section III

CONTROLS AND OPERATION

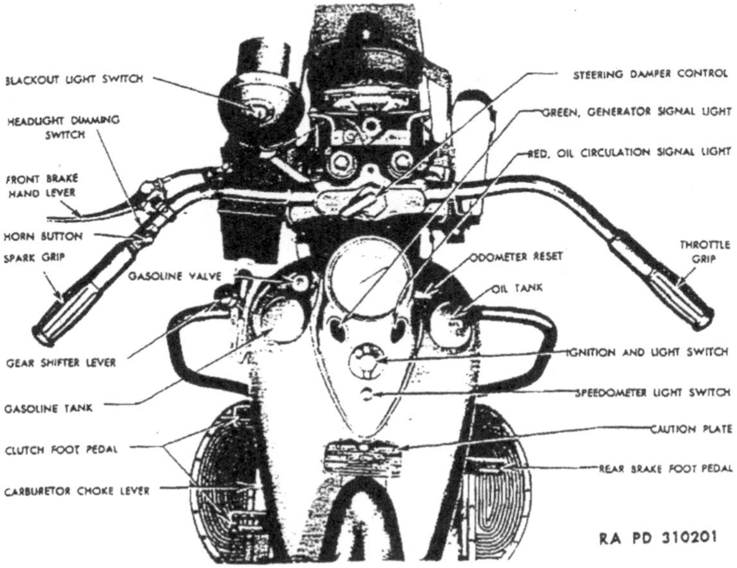

Figure 4—Controls

5. CONTROLS (fig. 4).

a. Controls are peculiar to the motorcycle. The rider must become thoroughly familiar with the location and use of all control devices before attempting to operate vehicle.

b. Gasoline Valve (figs. 5 and 6). Gasoline valve is located in left tank, forward. Valve is closed by turning to the right, finger tight. Turning to left opens valve. Valve is in normal operating position

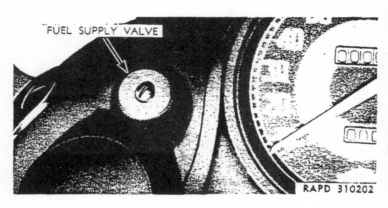

Figure 5—Fuel Supply Valve

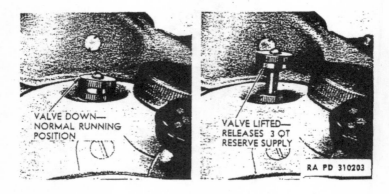

Figure 6—Fuel Supply Valve Positions

when turned to left, with valve head down. Lifting valve head releases emergency supply of fuel (3 quarts).

    c. Throttle. The throttle is controlled by right handle bar grip. Turning grip inward opens throttle, turning it outward closes throttle.

    d. Spark. Spark is controlled by left handle bar grip. Turning grip inward advances spark, turning it outward retards spark.

    e. Clutch (fig. 7). Clutch is operated by left foot (rocker-type) pedal, connecting with steel cable, which actuates clutch release lever. Pedal is located on left side of motorcycle above footboard. Forward downward (toe) position of pedal engages clutch. Rear downward (heel) position of pedal disengages clutch. Foot pedal provided with friction device to retain it in either engaged or disengaged position.

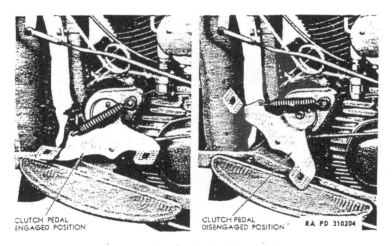

Figure 7—Clutch Pedal Positions

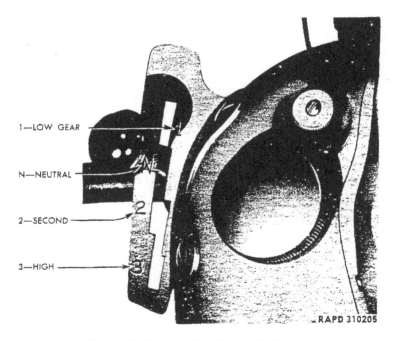

Figure 8—Gear Shifter Lever Positions

f. **Service Brake** (Rear Wheel). Foot pedal is located on right side of motorcycle at forward end of footboard.

g. **Auxiliary Brake** (Front Wheel). Auxiliary brake is operated by hand lever located on left handle bar. It is used in conjunction with service brake, as an emergency brake, or for holding vehicle while starting engine on grade. CAUTION: *Brake is to be applied lightly and cautiously on wet and slippery roads.*

h. **Gear Shifter** (fig. 8). Shifter lever is located on left tank, forward position, and operates within a guide. Shifter lever guide is notched for positive location of gears and each position is identified, front to rear: "1"—low gear; "N"—neutral; "2"—second gear; "3"—direct high gear.

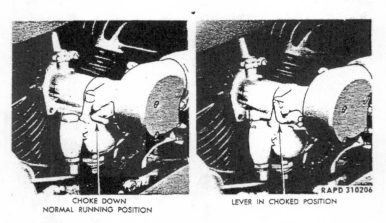

CHOKE DOWN
NORMAL RUNNING POSITION

LEVER IN CHOKED POSITION

RAPD 310206

Figure 9—Carburetor Choke Lever Positions

i. **Steering Damper.** Steering damper is an adjustable friction device to damper turning action of forks, steady front wheel, and prevent wobble in rough terrain or at high speeds, and is located on top of steering head in center of handle bars. Move handle to right to apply desired friction.

j. **Foot Starter Crank** (fig. 1). The foot starter crank is located on right side of motorcycle. Gear shifter lever must be in neutral position, and clutch foot pedal in forward engaged position, before using foot starter crank. Starter crank normally is in upward position. Straddle motorcycle, place right foot on starter crank, and shift weight of body for forceful downward crank operation to start engine.

k. **Ignition and Light Switch.** Earlier models are provided with switch lock, later models are nonlocking. Switch is off in straightforward position. First position to right is for engine ignition only.

Second position to right is for ignition and blackout lights. To use
vehicle service lights, depress button to turn switch to third right
position.

l.   **Instrument Panel Signal Lights.** Instead of an ammeter and
oil pressure gage, signal lights indicate generator charging, and engine
oil pressure.

(1)   Green light is located on left side of instrument panel. When
engine is running, and light is out, it indicates generator is charging.

(2)   Red light is located on right side of instrument panel. When
engine is running, and light is out, it indicates engine oil is circulating.

m.   **Carburetor Choke** (fig. 9). Choke lever is in full prime position when all the way up, and in normal running position when all
the way down.

6.   ENGINE PRESTARTING INSTRUCTIONS.

a.   Before the engine is started, perform the Before-operation Service outlined in paragraph 15. Special care must be taken during
starting and warming-up period to avoid unnecessary engine wear.

b.   The rider must acquire correct motorcycle engine starting
habits, and learn to do the job the quickest, easiest, and most dependable way. The following pointers will be helpful to the beginner as
well as to a seasoned rider:

(1)   Mount (straddle) motorcycle to obtain firm grip on handle
bars.

(2)   Leave side stand (jiffy stand) outward to support vehicle
while operating foot starter crank with right foot.

(3)   Engine starting will be benefited by use of front wheel, hand-
operated brake, to prevent vehicle from rolling or shifting during
starting kicks. This is especially helpful if vehicle is parked on an
incline or on soft, uneven surface.

c.   The procedure outlined below is preparatory to starting either
cold, warm, or hot engine:

(1)   Place gear shifter lever in "N" (neutral) position (fig. 8).

(2)   See that gasoline shut-off valve is open (fig. 5).

(3)   Engage clutch (fig. 7).

(4)   Spark control (left) grip must be turned inward to fully
advanced position, or nearly so.

(5)   Foot starter crank may travel ½ way downward before starting engine. See that a full vigorous starter stroke is used. A vigorous
kick, using a full swing (not a jab) of right leg and hip, is correct
engine starting practice.

7. STARTING THE ENGINE.

a. Procedure for starting cold. warm, or hot motorcycle engines differs. Therefore. following instructions are used with paragraph 6 c to cover correct procedure in all three cases.

b. **Starting Cold Engine.** When vehicle has not been operated for some time, and engine is normally cold. follow progressive procedure for easiest starting.

(1) Set carburetor choke lever in full upward (closed) position.

(2) Open throttle wide by turning right grip inward as far as it will go.

(3) Prime cylinders by operating foot starter crank one or two strokes.

(4) Set carburetor choke lever in $\frac{1}{4}$ to $\frac{1}{2}$ closed position for mild weather starting: $\frac{3}{4}$ closed (or leave fully choked) for extremely cold weather starting. CAUTION: *It is only in extremely cold weather that engine may start best with choke fully closed, and even then it will have to be moved from this position immediately after engine is started.*

(5) Set throttle (right) grip to slightly open position.

(6) Turn ignition switch on, first right position.

(7) Start engine with vigorous strokes of foot starter crank.

(8) When engine starts, set throttle for moderate idling speed for warming up. or until ready to set vehicle in motion. Do not race engine unnecessarily.

(9) After engine warms up, and misfires due to an overrich mixture, gradually move choke lever downward. After engine has thoroughly warmed up, move choke lever to fully open (downward) position.

c. **Starting Warm Engine.** Following instructions apply to engine when halfway between hot and cold. With engine in this condition, carburetor choking must be handled cautiously.

(1) Lift choke lever to first upward position from normal ($\frac{1}{4}$ closed).

(2) Set throttle (right) grip to fully closed (outward) position.

(3) Operate foot starter crank one or two strokes.

(4) Set throttle grip to between $\frac{1}{4}$ and $\frac{1}{3}$ open position.

(5) Turn ignition switch on.

(6) Start engine with vigorous strokes of foot starter crank.

(7) Soon after engine starts, choke lever must be moved to fully open (downward) position.

(8) Turn throttle grip to control idling speed of engine.

d. **Starting Hot Engine.** If engine has been shut off for only a brief period and is near normal operating temperature, it is not necessary to use carburetor choke lever. With some engines, depending upon carburetor condition and adjustment, hot starting is easier and more dependable if foot starter crank is operated one stroke before turning ignition switch on.

(1) Close throttle grip by turning fully outward.

(2) Turn ignition switch on.

(3) Operate foot starter crank to start engine.

(4) When hot engine does not start readily after two or three strokes of the foot starter crank, it is usually due to an overrich (flooded) condition, and the proper procedure then is to open throttle wide so that more air can enter; close throttle quickly after engine starts. CAUTION: *After engine has warmed up to a normal operating temperature, do not allow engine to stand idling for longer than a 1-minute interval.*

e. **Starting Engine with Dead Battery.** See paragraph 12.

f. **Behavior of Instrument Panel Signal Lights.** Function of generator (green) signal light depends upon action of cut-out relay; engine oil pressure (red) signal light depends upon action of oil feed pump. Rider must, therefore, thoroughly understand operating characteristics of both signal lights to judge condition of generator-battery circuit and pressure in engine oil circulating system.

(1) When ignition light switch is turned to first (right) position, preparatory to starting engine, both green and red signal lights should go on. CAUTION: *When switch is turned on, immediately after engine has been primed by cranking, red (oil pressure) signal light may not light at once, but will light after a few seconds, due to oil pressure built up by cranking, and is most likely to be noticed in cold weather.*

(2) With engine started and running at medium idling speed, both signal lights should go off. CAUTION: *Should oil pressure (red) signal light fail to go off at speeds above idling, conditions must be brought to attention of unit mechanic.*

(3) At slow idle speed, or under approximately 20 miles per hour road speed (in high gear), generator (green) signal light will normally flash on and off, because at that speed generator voltage output is very low and unsteady. CAUTION: *Should generator (green) signal light fail to go off at speed above approximately 20 miles per hour, generator is either not charging at all, or its current output is not up to normal, and generator should be given attention at once.*

8. STOPPING THE ENGINE.

a. Stop engine only by turning ignition and light switch to off (straight-ahead) position, to prevent discharge of battery through spark coil primary circuit.

9. OPERATION OF VEHICLE.

a. **Starting on Level Ground.** The engine having been warmed up and checked for satisfactory operation, the vehicle (with operator in riding position) is put in motion as follows:

(1) Transfer body weight to right leg.

(2) Fold back side stand (jiffy stand).

(3) Disengage clutch by depressing clutch foot pedal with heel of left foot.

(4) Shift gear shifter lever into "1" (low) gear position.

(5) Slowly engage clutch by depressing clutch foot pedal with toe of left foot.

(6) When clutch starts to "take hold," open throttle sufficiently to maintain engine speed.

(7) Accelerate gradually to between 12 and 15 miles per hour in low gear.

(8) Close throttle quickly.

(9) Disengage clutch.

(10) Shift through "N" (neutral) position into "2" (second) gear.

(11) Reengage clutch and accelerate to about 25 miles per hour.

(12) Close throttle quickly.

(13) Disengage clutch.

(14) Shift into "3" (high) gear.

(15) Reengage clutch and accelerate to desired speed.

b. **Starting on Uneven or Soft Ground.**

(1) If standing on an incline or in loose, heavy ground, more engine power will be required to start vehicle without stalling engine.

(2) It may be necessary to keep vehicle from rolling by keeping pressure on front brake hand lever. Brake pressure is released after vehicle starts in forward motion.

(3) Open throttle and engage clutch at same time to provide power needed for starting, without racing engine unnecessarily.

(4) Motorcycle starts should be made without excessive application of power, with consequent unnecessary spinning of rear wheel.

10. DRIVING PRECAUTIONS.

a. Practice will enable a rider to judge at what rate of speed the motorcycle should be moving before he shifts from a lower to higher gear. and engine should never be permitted to labor unduly, when a shift of gears. higher to lower. would improve operation.

(1) Operator must not look down at gear shifter when shifting gears. but keep his eyes on the road ahead. Do not ride the clutch. The operator's foot should rest on clutch foot pedal only when he is operating it. When shifting gears. disengage clutch fully to avoid gear damage and shifting difficulties. CAUTION: *Many transmissions are ruined through failure to disengage clutch fully when shifting gears.*

b. Braking. Rear wheel service brake must be in such condition that medium-hard application will cause rear wheel to lock. Application of service brake should be gradual, with just enough force to accomplish desired result.

(1) Auxiliary front wheel brake. when used in conjunction with service brake. must be applied with caution, especially on wet, muddy. or slippery roads.

(2) After passing through water, the brakes should be set slightly. and the vehicle operated for a short distance, until sufficient heat has been generated to dry the brakes.

c. Avoid Low Gear Operation. Always operate vehicle in highest gear possible, consistent with tactical situation, speed required. power required. and kind and nature of road substance, to prevent overheating of engine.

d. High Speed Tips. Only experienced riders should indulge in high-speed riding. A motorcycle operated for long distances at high speed must be given closer than ordinary attention to avoid serious engine overheating with consequent damage. For better motorcycle service. apply the following suggestions:

(1) Develop habit of frequently snapping throttle shut for an instant when running at high speed. This draws additional lubrication to piston and cylinder and assists in cooling engine.

(2) In cool weather. operate engine slowly until it is thoroughly warmed up. to avoid. damage to pistons. rings. cylinders. and other parts before oil is warm enough to circulate freely.

(3) If handle bar windshield and leg shields are used. engine is more likely to overheat with continued high-speed riding. Watch this carefully.

(4) Adjust "steering damper" for best control of motorcycle consistent with riding speed and condition and nature of road.

11. STOPPING AND PARKING VEHICLE.

a. Stopping Vehicle. Rider will make a "restart" easier and quicker if he will apply the following instructions upon stopping vehicle:

(1)   Close throttle.

(2)   Disengage clutch.

(3)   Apply brake (or brakes) to slow vehicle without sliding rear tire.

(4)   Just before coming to a complete stop, shift into "N" (neutral) position and engage clutch. CAUTION: *If immediate restart is to be made, shift into "1" (low) gear and allow clutch foot pedal to remain in disengaged position. (Rider will be mounted on motorcycle with engine running.)*

(5)   Continue brake application to complete stop.

(6)   After vehicle slows to point where it can no longer be balanced by steering, place left foot on ground to maintain balance until right foot can be removed from brake operating pedal. CAUTION: *Do not idle engine longer than 1 minute.*

(7)   Stop engine by turning ignition switch off.

b.   **Parking Vehicle.**

(1)   Lean motorcycle on side (jiffy) stand.

(2)   Shift into "1" (low) gear.

(3)   Engage clutch so vehicle cannot roll.

(4)   Shut off gasoline supply by turning valve (to right) finger-tight against its seat.

12.   TOWING VEHICLE TO START ENGINE.

a.   In emergencies when engine cannot be started with foot starter crank, it can be started by towing the motorcycle.

(1)   Set gear shifter lever in "2" (second) gear position.

(2)   Disengage clutch.

(3)   Choke carburetor.

(4)   Turn ignition switch on.

(5)   After momentum of the towed motorcycle reaches between 10 and 15 miles per hour, engage clutch, and continue procedure until engine starts.

b.   **Engine Starting with Dead Battery.** Emergency engine starting with dead battery can be effected by making use of freshly charged battery, or by towing as outlined above. If vehicle with dead battery is to be towed for engine starting, proceed as follows:

(1)   Disconnect battery negative wire from ground on right side of motorcycle.

(2)   Tow motorcycle for engine starting.

(3)   After engine is started, reconnect battery ground wire to frame to prevent damage to electrical system.

13.   RUNNING-IN NEW ENGINE (OR VEHICLE).

a.   A new motorcycle engine or newly overhauled engine must be given proper "break-in" consideration for at least the first 1.000 to 1.200 miles of service. Failure to do this may result in damage that will put engine out of active service within a short period of time.

b.   At the first 250 miles. check front and rear drive chains to make sure they are receiving required amount of oil for ample lubrication. If necessary. have chain oilers adjusted by unit mechanic. Drive chains must be inspected for correct adjustment. and be given attention by unit mechanic as needed.

c.   At first 500 miles. drain oil tank and refill with fresh oil. Check front and rear chains (step b above). Thereafter. follow instructions in Maintenance Operation section.

d.   After a new motorcycle has been run 500 to 1.000 miles it needs to be thoroughly checked over and any loose screws and nuts tightened. Particular attention must be given engine and transmission mounting bolts and nuts, and to rear wheel mounting socket screws.

e.   Following pointers must be observed when running-in new engine or newly overhauled engine:

(1)   Do not exceed 30 miles per hour during first 100 miles.

(2)   Do not exceed 35 miles per hour during next 200 miles.

(3)   Do not exceed 40 miles per hour during next 400 miles.

(4)   Do not exceed 50 miles per hour during next 500 miles.

(5)   Avoid use of low gears during break-in operation as much as possible.

FIRST ECHELON PREVENTIVE MAINTENANCE SERVICES

14. PURPOSE.

a. To insure mechanical efficiency it is necessary that the vehicle be systematically inspected at intervals each day it is operated and weekly, so that defects may be discovered and corrected before they result in serious damage or failure. Certain scheduled maintenance services will be performed at these designated intervals. The services set forth in this section are those performed by driver or crew before operation, during operation, at halt, after operation, and weekly.

h. Driver preventive maintenance services are listed on the back of "Driver's Trip Ticket and Preventive Maintenance Service Record," W.D. Form No. 48, to cover vehicles of all types and models. Items peculiar to specific vehicles, but not listed on W.D. Form No. 48, are covered in manual procedures under the items to which they are related. Certain items listed on the form that do not pertain to the vehicle involved are eliminated from the procedures as written into the manual. Every organization must thoroughly school each driver in performing the maintenance procedures set forth in manuals, whether or not they are listed specifically on W.D. Form No. 48.

c. The items listed on W.D. Form No. 48 that apply to this vehicle are expanded in this manual to provide specific procedures for accomplishment of the inspections and services. These services are arranged to facilitate inspection and conserve the time of the driver, and are not necessarily in the same numerical order as shown on W.D. Form No. 48. The item numbers, however, are identical with those shown on that form.

d. The general inspection of each item applies also to any supporting member or connection, and generally includes a check to see whether the item is in good condition, correctly assembled, secure, or excessively worn.

(1) The inspection for "good condition" is usually an external visual inspection to determine whether the unit is damaged beyond safe or serviceable limits. The term "good condition" is explained further by the following: not bent or twisted, not chafed or burned,

not broken or cracked, not bare or frayed, not dented or collapsed, not torn or cut.

(2)   The inspection of a unit to see that it is "correctly assembled" is usually an external visual inspection to see whether it is in its normal assembled position in the vehicle.

(3)   The inspection of a unit to determine if it is "secure" is usually an external visual examination, a hand-feel, or a pry-bar check for looseness. Such an inspection should include any brackets, lock washers, lock nuts, locking wires, or cotter pins used in assembly.

(4)   "Excessively worn" will be understood to mean worn close to, or beyond, serviceable limits, and likely to result in a failure if not replaced before the next scheduled inspection.

e.   Any defects or unsatisfactory operating characteristics beyond the scope of first echelon to correct must be reported at the earliest opportunity to the designated individual in authority.

15.   BEFORE-OPERATION SERVICE.

a.   This inspection schedule is designed primarily as a check to see that the vehicle has not been tampered with, or sabotaged since the After-operation Service was performed. Various combat conditions may have rendered the vehicle unsafe for operation and it is the duty of the driver to determine whether or not the vehicle is in condition to carry out any mission to which it is assigned. This operation will not be entirely omitted, even in extreme tactical situations.

b.   **Procedures.** Before-operation Service consists of inspecting items listed below according to the procedure described, and correcting or reporting any deficiencies. Upon completion of the service, results should be reported promptly to the designated individual in authority.

(1)   ITEM 1, TAMPERING AND DAMAGE. Look for any injury to vehicle in general, its accessories or equipment, that may have been caused by tampering, sabotage, collision, falling debris, or shell fire since parking vehicle. Look for loosened or damaged accessories, loose fuel or oil lines, or any disconnected linkage.

(2)   ITEM 3, FUEL AND OIL. Inspect tanks for fuel and oil levels, add oil and fuel as necessary. Any appreciable change in levels since performing After-operation Service should be investigated and reported to designated authority.

(3)   ITEM 4, ACCESSORIES AND DRIVES. Examine all accessories such as carburetor, air cleaner, generator, and cut-out relay for loose connections, loose mountings, or leaks. Examine rear chain (final drive) for free up-and-down movement (slack), midway between sprockets. Total up-and-down movement must not be more than 1 inch, nor less than $\frac{1}{2}$ inch. Inspect rear chain for adequate lubrication.

(4) ITEM 6, LEAKS, GENERAL. Examine vehicle and ground under vehicle for indications of fuel or oil leaks. Normally a few drops of waste oil from chains may be expected to drop from skid plate.

(5) ITEM 11, GLASS. Clean glass on instruments; clean and adjust rear view mirror; inspect glass for breakage.

(6) ITEM 12, LAMPS. If tactical situation permits, observe whether blackout and service lights operate with switch in its respective positions, and go out when switched off. Also see that lights are secure, and that lenses are clean and not broken. Observe whether both filaments of service headlight operate when dimmer switch on left handle bar is moved to its respective positions.

(7) ITEM 13, WHEELS, AXLE NUTS AND SCREWS. Examine rear wheel mounting socket screws, front and rear axle nuts, and front fork rocker stud nuts for tightness. Observe rear chain adjusting screws for secure locking. Inspect spokes for good condition and tightness.

(8) ITEM 14, TIRES. Examine tires for cuts or imbedded objects in treads or carcass. If time permits, check air pressure, which should be 18 pounds front, and 20 pounds rear (tires cold). Inspect valve caps for presence and secure mounting.

(9) ITEM 15, SPRINGS AND SUSPENSION. Examine front fork springs for secure mounting and good condition. Push down rear of saddle to test for full action of saddle post spring.

(10) ITEM 16, STEERING AND HANDLE BAR CONTROLS. Test steering head bearing adjustment by exerting strong upward pull at handle bar grips, and observing whether or not there is any noticeable play in bearing. Operate steering damper lever and observe that damper is compressed before lever reaches right-side position, and is fully released with lever in left-side position. Test handle bar grip controls for full, free action; also test for complete opening and closing of throttle, and full advance and retard of timer.

(11) ITEM 17, FENDERS (MUDGUARDS), LUGGAGE CARRIER, SAFETY GUARDS, AND STANDS. Examine these items for good condition and secure mounting.

(12) ITEM 21, TOOLS AND EQUIPMENT. Inspect tools and equipment for presence, serviceability, and proper stowage. (See tool list in par. 21.)

(13) ITEM 7, ENGINE WARM-UP. Start engine, noting any tendency toward hard starting, or improper action of foot starter crank. Set throttle to moderate idle speed. Listen for unusual noises. Watch instrument indications and engine performance, such as misfiring. CAUTION: *Do not idle engine longer than 1 minute with vehicle standing.*

(14) ITEM 8, CHOKE. During idling of engine. reset choke as required to prevent excessive choking and dilution of engine oil.

(15) ITEM 9, INSTRUMENTS. When switch is turned on and engine is idling at moderate speed both red light (indicating oil pressure) and green light (indicating generator action) should be out. At lower operating speeds generator-indicating light may flicker. CAUTION: *Do not operate engine with red light on (no oil pressure).*

(16) ITEM 10, HORN. Tactical situation permitting, test horn.

(17) ITEM 22, ENGINE OPERATION. Engine should idle smoothly. Accelerate and decelerate. listening for any unusual noises that may indicate compression or exhaust leaks, worn, damaged, loose, or inadequately lubricated engine parts, or accessories. Note any unusual smoke from exhaust.

(18) ITEM 23, DRIVER'S PERMIT, ACCIDENT REPORT FORM NO. 26, AND VEHICLE MANUAL. These items must be present on vehicle and safely stowed.

(19) ITEM 25, DURING-OPERATION SERVICE. The During-operation Service should start immediately after vehicle is put in motion. in the nature of a road test.

16. DURING-OPERATION SERVICE.

a. While vehicle is in motion, listen for any sounds such as rattles. knocks, squeals, or hums that may indicate trouble. Be alert to detect any odor of overheated components or units such as generator. brakes, or clutch, fuel vapor from a leak in fuel system, exhaust gas. or other signs of trouble. Any time the brakes are used, gears shifted, or vehicle turned, consider this a test and notice any unsatisfactory or unusual performance. Watch the instruments constantly. Notice promptly any unusual instrument indication that may signify possible trouble in system to which the instrument applies.

b. **Procedures.** During-operation Service consists of observing items listed below according to the procedures following each item. and investigating any indications of serious trouble. Notice minor deficiencies to be corrected or reported at earliest opportunity, usually at next scheduled halt.

(1) ITEM 27, FOOT AND HAND BRAKES. The foot brake should operate smoothly and effectively, leaving reserve pedal travel of 1 inch. Normal free play before operation is 1 inch. Test hand brake lever for free play, which should be $\frac{1}{4}$ of total handle travel. Test for ease and smoothness of operation.

(2) ITEM 28, CLUTCH. Inspect clutch for disengagement at about $\frac{1}{2}$ pedal travel. Clutch should not chatter, squeal, or slip.

(3) ITEM 29, TRANSMISSION. Gears should shift smoothly, operate quietly, and not jump out of mesh during operation. If transmission

jumps out of mesh in any gear, this indicates need of shifter control adjustment.

(4)   ITEM 31, ENGINE AND CONTROLS. Be alert for deficiency in engine performance such as lack of usual power. misfiring, unusual noise, stalling, indication of engine overheating, or unusual exhaust smoke. Notice whether engine responds to controls satisfactorily, whether controls appear to be in proper adjustment and are sufficiently tight.

(5)   ITEM 32, INSTRUMENTS. Observe instruments for indication of normal functioning of systems to which they apply.

(a)   Speedometer and Odometer. Speedometer should indicate vehicle speed without excessive noise or fluctuation. Odometer should record trip and total mileage.

(b)   Oil Pressure Signal Light. Red light should be off during operation. If light goes on, stop vehicle and investigate for oil pressure failure.

(c)   Generator Signal Light. Green light should be off above 20 miles per hour. Battery discharge is indicated by green light being on.

(6)   ITEM 33, STEERING. Adjust steering damper to desired steering friction. Observe vehicle steering for wander, shimmy, leading to one side, or wheel hop.

(7)   ITEM 34, RUNNING GEAR. Listen for any unusual noises from wheels, axles, or suspension parts that might indicate looseness or damage.

(8)   ITEM 35, CHASSIS. Be alert for noises that might indicate loose accessories, controls, attachments, or equipment.

17.   AT-HALT SERVICE.

a.   At-halt Service may be regarded as minimum maintenance procedures and should be performed under all tactical conditions, even though more extensive maintenance services must be slighted or omitted altogether.

b.   **Procedures.** At-halt Service consists of investigating any deficiencies noted during operation, inspecting items listed below according to the procedures following the items, and correcting any deficiencies found. Deficiencies not corrected should be reported promptly to the designated individual in authority.

(1)   ITEM 38, FUEL AND OIL. Replenish fuel and oil as may be required to reach next refilling point. CAUTION: *Left tank is for fuel; right tank is for oil. Filler caps should not be interchanged, as only fuel tank cap is vented.*

(2)   ITEM 39, TEMPERATURES. Hand-feel wheel hubs and brake drums for overheating.

(3) ITEM 40, VENTS. Make sure that crankcase breather outlet and rear chain oil feed pipe are clear. Make sure grease drains in front and rear brake side covers are open and clean.

(4) ITEM 42, SPRINGS AND SUSPENSIONS. Look for broken springs in fork.

(5) ITEM 43, STEERING. Investigate any difficulty developed during riding.

(6) ITEM 44, WHEELS AND MOUNTING SCREWS. Inspect wheels for broken, bent, or loose spokes. Also, look for loose axle nuts or rear wheel mounting screws. Inspect wheel rims for good condition.

(7) ITEM 45, TIRES. Examine tires for low pressure or damage. Remove foreign matter from tire treads; inspect for cuts.

(8) ITEM 46, LEAKS, GENERAL. Inspect vehicle for indication of fuel, oil, or battery leaks.

(9) ITEM 47, ACCESSORIES AND CHAIN. Examine accessories for loose connections, loose mountings, or damage. Examine rear drive chain for broken rollers, broken link side plates, and broken or missing connecting link spring clips. Inspect chain for adequate lubrication.

(10) ITEM 48, AIR CLEANER. Air cleaner must be secure, with air passages in good condition and clean. When operating under extremely dusty or sandy conditions, inspect air cleaner frequently and service as required.

(11) ITEM 49, FENDERS (MUDGUARDS), LUGGAGE CARRIER, SAFETY GUARDS, AND STANDS. Inspect these items for looseness or damage.

(12) ITEM 52, APPEARANCE AND GLASS. Clean windshield, rear view mirror, and light lenses; inspect for good condition, secure attachment, and broken glass.

18. AFTER-OPERATION AND WEEKLY SERVICE.

a. After-operation Service is particularly important, because at this time the driver inspects his vehicle to detect any deficiencies that may have developed, and corrects those he is permitted to handle. He should report promptly, to the designated individual in authority, the results of his inspection. If this schedule is performed thoroughly, the vehicle should be ready to roll again on a moment's notice. The Before-operation Service, with a few exceptions, is then necessary only to ascertain whether the vehicle is in the same condition in which it was left upon completion of the After-operation Service. The After-operation Service should never be entirely omitted, even in extreme tactical situations, but may be reduced to the bare fundamental services outlined for the At-halt Service, if necessary.

b. Procedures. When performing the After-operation Service, the driver must remember and consider any irregularities noticed during the day in the Before-operation, During-operation, and At-halt Services. The After-operation Service consists of inspecting and servicing the following items. Those items of the After-operation Services that are marked with an asterisk (*) require additional Weekly services, the procedures for which are indicated in step *(b)* of each applicable item.

(1) ITEM 54, FUEL AND OIL. Fill fuel and oil tanks; fill oil tank within 1 inch of top; be sure to put oil in right tank and fuel in left tank; do not interchange caps. CAUTION: *When operating under extremely dusty conditions, drain engine oil tank and refill with fresh oil as frequently as excessive contamination of the oil occurs.*

(2) ITEM 55, ENGINE OPERATION. Test for satisfactory engine idle without stalling. Accelerate and decelerate engine, noting any tendency to miss or backfire, unusual noises, or vibration that may indicate worn parts, loose mounting, incorrect fuel mixture, or faulty ignition. Investigate any unsatisfactory engine operating characteristics noted during operation. Learn to recognize noise caused by loose primary (front) drive chain. Slack in excess of $\frac{1}{2}$ inch total up-and-down motion can cause excessive noise which sounds like engine knock. Remove inspection cover for examination of chain.

(3) ITEM 57, HORN. If tactical situation permits, test horn.

(4) ITEM 59, LIGHTS. If tactical situation permits, observe whether blackout and service lights operate with switch in its respective positions, and go out when switched off. Also see that lights are secure, and lenses clean and not broken. Observe whether both filaments of service headlight operate when dimmer switch on left handle bar is moved to its respective positions.

(5) ITEM 56, INSTRUMENTS. Before stopping engine, inspect instruments to see that indicator lights are still out. Stop engine. After 30 seconds, turn on switch to see that oil pressure and generator signal lights turn on. CAUTION: *Be sure to turn off ignition switch after this test.*

(6) ITEM 58, GLASS. Clean rear view mirror, windshield, instrument, and light glass. Examine for secure mounting and breakage.

(7) ITEM 62, *BATTERY.

(a) Inspect battery carrier for good condition and secure mounting. Inspect electrolyte level (should be $\frac{5}{16}$ inch above plates). Inspect for any signs of leakage of electrolyte indicating battery has been overfilled, poorly sealed, or damaged. CAUTION: *Do not add water unless actually needed.*

(b) *Weekly.* Clean dirt from top of battery, remove battery caps, bring electrolyte level to $\frac{5}{16}$ inch above plates, using clean, drinkable water. Clean terminals or posts if corroded; be sure felt washers are

on terminals and properly oiled; tighten terminal bolts cautiously, if loose. Clean and paint battery carrier if corroded.

(8) ITEM 63, *ACCESSORIES AND CHAIN.

(a) Inspect carburetor, air cleaner, generator, and cut-out relay for loose connections, mountings, or damage. Examine rear drive chain for broken rollers, broken link side plates, and broken or missing connecting link spring clips. Examine rear chain (final drive) for free up-and-down movement (slack) midway between sprockets; maximum total allowable deflection is 1 inch, minimum, $\frac{1}{2}$ inch.

(b) Weekly. Tighten any accessory connections found loose. Wipe excess dirt from rear chain. Check front chain for adjustment, and inspect for proper lubrication.

(9) ITEM 65, *AIR CLEANER.

(a) Examine oil cup for excessive dirt and correct oil level. If air cleaner is excessively dirty, clean elements in dry-cleaning solvent, refill cup with fresh oil. Dip elements in oil in oil cup, replacing elements and attaching oil cup immediately. If gaskets are damaged, replace. Under extremely dusty or sandy conditions it may be necessary to clean and refill the air cleaner more than once daily. Inspect hose for leaks.

(b) Weekly. Inspect air cleaner for proper oil level and excessively dirty oil. Clean and service air cleaner, tighten mounting and hose clamps. NOTE: *Early-type, round air cleaner does not have removable filter elements. Complete cleaner must be removed to wash element.*

(10) ITEM 66, *FUEL FILTER (GASOLINE STRAINER).

(a) Clean cap and screen of fuel filter.

(b) Weekly. Clean cap and screen of fuel filter, remove carburetor bowl drain plug, and drain off water and dirt. Be sure to replace plug, being careful to avoid cross threading.

(11) ITEM 67, ENGINE CONTROLS. Examine throttle and spark controls for damage to wires or for disconnected linkage. Observe for lack of lubrication.

(12) ITEM 68, *TIRES.

(a) Remove foreign matter such as nails, glass, or stones from tire treads. Inspect tires for abnormal tread wear, cuts, or bruises; also for presence and tightness of valve caps. Inflate tires to 18 pounds front, 20 pounds rear, with tires cool.

(b) Weekly. Replace badly worn or otherwise unserviceable tires.

(13) ITEM 69, *SPRINGS AND SUSPENSION.

(a) Inspect front fork for broken or sagged springs, loose bolts, studs, and nuts.

(b) Weekly. Tighten wheel axle nuts and rear brake sleeve nut. Also tighten rear wheel mounting socket screws very securely.

(14) ITEM 70, STEERING. Inspect steering head for proper adjustment of bearings. Examine steering damper for correct adjustment.

(15) ITEM 72, *VENTS.

(a) Make sure that crankcase breather outlet and rear chain oil supply pipe are clear. Make sure grease drains in front and rear brake side covers are open and clean.

(b) Weekly. Clean crankcase breather outlet, rear chain oil supply pipe, and grease drains in front and rear brake side covers.

(16) ITEM 73, LEAKS, GENERAL. Look around mechanism and beneath vehicle for indication of fuel, oil, and grease leaks. Examine around brake drums for evidence of grease in drums or on linings. Normally a few drops of oil may be expected to drip from skid plate.

(17) ITEM 74, GEAR OIL LEVELS. Inspect transmission oil level with vehicle standing on rear stand (not jiffy stand); refill, if required, to level of filler plug opening with engine oil. CAUTION: *Do not use gear oil.*

(18) ITEM 76, FENDERS (MUDGUARDS), LUGGAGE CARRIER, SAFETY GUARDS, AND STANDS. Examine these items for good condition and secure mounting.

(19) ITEM 82, *TIGHTEN.

(a) Inspect all frame and assembly nuts, bolts, and cap screws for tightness.

(b) Weekly. Tighten all vehicle assembly or mounting nuts. Driver is cautioned not to tamper with or tighten screws or nuts about the circuit breaker, as doing so may disturb ignition timing.

(20) ITEM 83, *LUBRICATE AS NEEDED.

(a) Lubricate all parts where inspection reveals need for lubrication; wipe all dirt from fittings before applying lubricant. Report any missing fittings.

(b) Weekly. When vehicle has been driven a sufficient number of miles so that it is due for a regularly scheduled lubrication, lubricate according to Lubrication Guide in manual and current lubrication directives. Refrain from overlubricating wheel bearings, front brake side cover bushing, and front and rear brake operating lever camshafts.

(21) ITEM 84, *CLEAN ENGINE AND VEHICLE.

(a) Clean dirt and trash from vehicle and remove excess grease.

(b) Weekly. Wash vehicle if possible. If not, wipe off thoroughly. Do not rub lustreless paint enough to cause shine. If vehicle is washed in a stream, care should be taken that water or dirt does not get into bearings, breather valve, or brakes. CAUTION: *It is extremely im-*

portant that high-pressure streams or steam should not be directed against wheel hubs, brakes, carburetor, air cleaner, or electrical units.

(22) ITEM 64, *ELECTRICAL WIRING.

(a) Inspect all ignition wiring to see that it is securely connected, clean, and not damaged.

(b) *Weekly*. Inspect all wiring to see that it is securely connected and supported, that insulation is not cracked or chafed, that loom, shielding, and condensers are in good condition and securely attached. Clean as required. Tighten any loose connections carefully. Radio shielding or bonding defects, except cleaning or tightening, must be referred to signal corps personnel.

(23) ITEM 85, *TOOLS AND EQUIPMENT.

(a) See that all tools and equipment assigned to vehicle are present, in good condition, and properly stowed.

(b) *Weekly*. Check tools and equipment assigned to vehicle with vehicle stowage list (par. 21) to see that they are present. Inspect tools for good condition and proper stowage. Report missing or unserviceable items to designated authority.

LUBRICATION

19. INTRODUCTION.

a. Lubrication is an essential part of preventive maintenance, determining to a great extent serviceability of parts and assemblies.

20. LUBRICATION GUIDE (fig. 10).

a. **General.** Lubrication instructions for this materiel are consolidated in a Lubrication Guide (fig. 10). These specify the points to be lubricated, the periods of lubrication, and the lubricant to be used. Intervals indicated on the guide are for normal service. For extreme conditions, high speed, heat, mud, snow, rough roads, dust, etc., change engine oil and lubricate more frequently. In addition to the items on the guide, brake, gear shifter, clutch control linkage, and hinges must be lubricated at frequent intervals.

b. **Supplies.** In the field it may not be possible to supply a complete assortment of lubricants called for by the Lubrication Guide to meet the recommendations. It will be necessary to make the best use of those available, subject to inspection by the officer concerned, in consultation with responsible ordnance personnel.

c. **Lubrication Notes.** The following notes apply to the Lubrication Guide (fig. 10). All note references in the guide itself are to the steps below having the corresponding number:

(1) BRAKE FITTINGS. Exercise caution when lubricating brake operating cams and front brake cover bushing, as excess grease working out of these bearings is likely to get onto brake lining, reducing brake efficiency. CAUTION: *When using air-operated grease gun, make sure not to overlubricate brake fittings.*

(2) BRAKE HAND LEVER OILCAN POINTS. Oil hand lever fittings and "oiler" mounted on cable housing. Oil front brake control cable at ends of control cable housing.

(3) GENERATOR COMMUTATOR END BEARING. Hand-pack with general purpose grease, No. 2, at temperatures above zero. Below zero, use lighter grease. This operation requires removal of generator end cover. Bearing outer grease retainer must be loosened and swung aside for access to bearing. If not convenient to grease bearing at specified intervals, at least lubricate with a few drops of engine oil applied to hole in outer grease retainer. Do not overlubricate. CAUTION: *Generator regulating brush plate must not be shifted while*

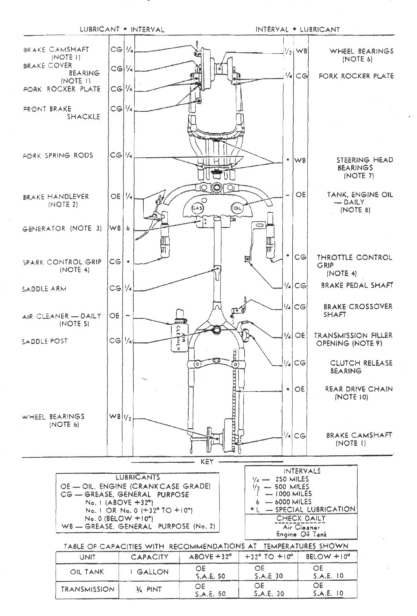

LUBRICANT • INTERVAL   INTERVAL • LUBRICANT

BRAKE CAMSHAFT (NOTE 1)	CG ¼	½ WB — WHEEL BEARINGS (NOTE 6)
BRAKE COVER BEARING (NOTE 11)	CG ¼	¼ CG — FORK ROCKER PLATE
FORK ROCKER PLATE	CG ¼	
FRONT BRAKE SHACKLE	CG ¼	
FORK SPRING RODS	CG ¼	• WB — STEERING HEAD BEARINGS (NOTE 7)
BRAKE HANDLEVER (NOTE 2)	OE ¼	- OE — TANK, ENGINE OIL — DAILY (NOTE 8)
GENERATOR (NOTE 3)	WB 6	
SPARK CONTROL GRIP (NOTE 4)	CG •	• CG — THROTTLE CONTROL GRIP (NOTE 4)
SADDLE ARM	CG ¼	¼ CG — BRAKE PEDAL SHAFT
AIR CLEANER — DAILY (NOTE 5)	OE -	¼ CG — BRAKE CROSSOVER SHAFT
SADDLE POST	CG ¼	¼ OE — TRANSMISSION FILLER OPENING (NOTE 9)
		¼ CG — CLUTCH RELEASE BEARING
		• OE — REAR DRIVE CHAIN (NOTE 10)
WHEEL BEARINGS (NOTE 6)	WB ½	
		¼ CG — BRAKE CAMSHAFT (NOTE 1)

— KEY —

LUBRICANTS
OE — OIL, ENGINE (CRANKCASE GRADE)
CG — GREASE, GENERAL PURPOSE
No. 1 (ABOVE +32°)
No. 1 OR No. 0 (+32° TO +10°)
No. 0 (BELOW +10°)
WB — GREASE, GENERAL PURPOSE (No. 2)

INTERVALS
¼ — 250 MILES
½ — 500 MILES
1 — 1000 MILES
6 — 6000 MILES
• L — SPECIAL LUBRICATION

CHECK DAILY
Air Cleaner
Engine Oil Tank

TABLE OF CAPACITIES WITH RECOMMENDATIONS AT TEMPERATURES SHOWN

UNIT	CAPACITY	ABOVE +32°	+32° TO +10°	BELOW +10°
OIL TANK	1 GALLON	OE S.A.E. 50	OE S.A.E 30	OE S.A.E. 10
TRANSMISSION	¾ PINT	OE S.A.E. 50	OE S.A.E. 30	OE S.A.E. 10

RA PD 310207

Figure 10—Lubrication Guide

bearing outer grease retainer is loose (par. 92). Generator drive end bearing requires no attention, since it is lubricated by oil circulating through engine.

(4) SPARK AND THROTTLE CONTROL GRIPS. These grips require disassembly. Twice a year, or whenever grips do not turn freely, indicating need of lubrication, remove grips, clean parts, apply grease, and reassemble (par. 101).

(5) AIR CLEANER. Examine oil cup daily for excessive dirt and correct oil level. Under extremely dusty or sandy conditions it may be necessary to clean and refill the air cleaner more than once daily. Refill oil cup to indicated level with engine oil. Drain, clean, and refill oil cup every 250 miles, depending upon operating conditions. Every 1,000 miles (oftener if necessary), remove air cleaner filter units, wash in dry-cleaning solvent, lubricate, and reassemble (par. 76). NOTE: *Early type round cleaner did not have removable filter element. Complete cleaner must be removed to wash element.*

(6) WHEEL BEARINGS. When wheel hubs are lubricated at regular 500-mile interval, ⅛ ounce of grease with each greasing is sufficient. This amounts to about 15 shots of the standard 1-pound air gun, or four strokes with a 1-pound, hand-operated gun. If vehicle has been operated in water, wheel hubs submerged, apply hub greasing service immediately afterward (or soon as situation permits). Do not over-lubricate wheel hub bearings, as excess grease may work into brake linings, reducing brake efficiency. When using air-operated grease gun, it is easy to overlubricate wheel hub bearings.

(7) STEERING HEAD BEARINGS. Every 50,000 miles, repack upper and lower bearings, or whenever there is occasion to remove rigid fork for repair or replacement (par. 98).

(8) TANK, ENGINE OIL. Oil tank is located on right side of motorcycle. Empty tank holds 1 U. S. gallon. Check daily and add engine oil as necessary to refill tank within 1 inch of top. Oil level gage rod (dip stick) is located directly below tank cap. When oil level is down to "REFILL" mark on gage rod, 2 U. S. quarts may be added. Drain oil tank every 1,000 miles and refill with fresh engine oil. Drain plug located on underside of tank in forward position. In extremely dusty service, and in winter weather, change oil oftener.

(a) *Winter Caution.* Water is a by-product of combustion in any internal combustion engine. In a condensed state, the water vapor formed would equal approximately the quantity of gasoline burned. Some of this water vapor escapes past the rings into the crankcase. When starting and warming up in cold weather, considerable vapor getting into crankcase condenses to water before crankcase is hot enough to exhaust the vapor, without inside condensation, through outside breather. If engine is driven enough to get crankcase thoroughly warmed up frequently, most of this water is again vaporized and blown out through outside breather. However, a moderately driven engine, making only short runs now and then, and seldom thoroughly warmed up, is likely to accumulate an increasing amount of water in oil tank. This water will, in freezing weather, become slush or ice and, if allowed to accumulate too long, may block oil lines with resulting damage to engine. Also, water mixed with oil for some time, forms a heavy sludge of considerable acid content that is very harmful to bearings and other internal engine parts. To sum it up briefly, an engine that is used only for short runs during freezing weather requires frequent oil changes along with thorough flushing of tank to remove any accumulated sludge.

(9) TRANSMISSION FILLER OPENING. Check oil level in transmission case every 250 miles and add engine oil as necessary to bring level up to filler opening. If motorcycle is run unusually long distances, inspect more frequently. Motorcycle must be on rear stand in straight upright position when checking oil level or filling transmission case. Use same grade of oil used in engine, summer, and winter. If gear shifting difficulty is caused by oil congealing in extremely cold weather, thin oil with small amount of kerosene or dry-cleaning solvent. Every 1,000 miles, drain and refill transmission to level of transmission filler plug opening with specified grade of engine oil. Transmission holds ¾ pint of oil. To drain transmission case remove filler plug and lay motorcycle on right side. CAUTION: *Do not leave motorcycle on side longer than two minutes.*

(10) DRIVE CHAINS.

(a) Front and rear drive chains are automatically supplied with lubrication by engine oil pumps. Chain oilers are adjustable and may need occasional readjustment to meet lubrication requirements of varied operating conditions. Every 1,000 miles (or more often if operating conditions are extremely severe) inspect front primary drive chain for adequate lubrication (fig. 36).

(b) At every 1,000-mile period rear drive chain should have additional lubrication as follows: Remove chain, wash thoroughly in dry-cleaning solvent and hang it up to dry. Then soak chain in SAE 10 engine oil for a short period of time to allow oil to penetrate into all chain bearings. Drain chain and wipe off excess oil. Install rear chain (par. 63). (This attention is not required by front chain.) Readjustment of chain oilers must be made only by organization mechanic (par. 61). CAUTION: *Inspect frequently and make sure that rear chain oiler supply pipe is clear, not bent or damaged.*

d. Before Applying Lubricant. Always wipe dirt from the lubrication fittings or plugs so that dirt will not enter with the lubricant Lubricate all chassis points after washing vehicle or after vehicle has been operated in streams or extremely muddy or slushy roads. CAU-TION: *It is extremely important that high-pressure cleaning streams*

*or steam should not be directed against ends of wheel hubs, brake
side cover bearings, air cleaner, handle bar grips, or electrical system.
To do so will seriously affect correct lubrication and functioning of
these parts.*

e. **Oilcan Points.** All brake, transmission, and clutch control
points not fitted with grease connections should be lubricated with
engine oil. Front brake control cable, spark, and throttle control
wires must be oiled at the ends of their respective housings, especially
after washing vehicle, or after operating it in wet weather. Keep
battery terminal felt washers saturated with engine oil to prevent
corrosion of connections.

f. **Warning Light.** Action of the engine oil feed pump is indicated
by red signal light in instrument panel. Rider must be thoroughly
familiar with operating characteristics of this signal light, to judge
condition of engine oil circulating system (par. 7 f).

TOOLS AND EQUIPMENT STOWAGE ON THE VEHICLE

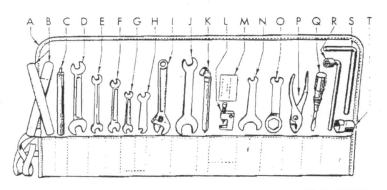

Figure 11—Vehicle Tools

21. VEHICLE TOOLS (fig. 11).

a. Kits. Included in the tool kit assembly are the following:

Legend Letter for Fig. 11	Tool	Number Carried	Mfr's Number	Federal Stock Number	Where Carried
A	Tool roll..............	1	11819-44	.....	In saddle bag
B	Irons, tire.............	2	11551-X	41-I-773-75	In tool roll
*C	Handle, chain tool.....	1	11817-40	41-H-1510-400	In tool roll
D	Wrench, ⅝-in. by ¾-in.	1	11804-44C	.....	In tool roll
E	Wrench, ½-in. by ⁹⁄₁₆-in.	1	11804-44B	.....	In tool roll
F	Wrench, ⁷⁄₁₆-in. by ½-in.	1	11804-44A	.....	In tool roll
G	Wrench, ⁵⁄₁₆-in. by ⅜-in.	1	11804-44	.....	In tool roll
H	Wrench, ⅜-in. by ⁷⁄₁₆-in. (valve tappet).......	1	11905-X	.....	In tool roll
I	Wrench, adjustable....	1	11813-44	.....	In tool roll
*J	Wrench, ¾-in. by 1¾-in. (rear axle nut and trans.)	1	11814-35	41-W-1989-850	In tool roll

*EXCEPTION: *Earlier models furnished with smaller tool roll and kit contain the items marked by asterisk.*

Legend Letter for Fig. 11	Tool	Number Carried	Mfr's Number	Federal Stock Number	Where Carried
K	Gage, tire............	1	11562-43	.....	In tool roll
*L	Tool, chain repair......	1	12039-38	.....	In tool roll
*M	Washers, 0.002-in. thick (chain oiler adj.).......	4	674-32	.....	In tool roll
*N	Wrench, ⁷⁄₁₆-in. by 1⅜-in. (vaive cover)..........	1	11806-31	41-W-3617	In tool roll
*O	Wrench, ⁵⁄₁₆-in. by 1⅛-in. (use with spark plug socket)...............	1	11929-39	.....	In tool roll
*P	Pliers, adjustable......	1	11812-44	.....	In tool roll
*Q	Screwdriver..........	1	11811-X	.....	In tool roll
R	Wrench, ⁹⁄₁₆-in. socket (cyl. head bolt)........	1	12047-30A	41-W01525	In tool roll
*S	Wrench, wheel mounting	1	11815-35	41-W-3825-400	In tool roll
*T	Wrench, socket (spark plug; use with O)	1	11805-40	41-W-3332	In tool roll
	Pump, tire...........	1	11553-41M	8-P-4900	On frame, left side
	Grease gun (in case)....	1	11661-38A	.....	In saddle bag

*EXCEPTION: *Earlier models furnished with smaller tool roll and kit contain the items marked by asterisk.*

22. VEHICLE EQUIPMENT (figs. 12 and 13).

a. Attached to Vehicle.

Item	Number Carried	Where Carried
Saddlebags	2	On luggage carrier
Mirror, rear view	1	On left handle bar
Box, submachine gun ammunition	1	Front fender, left side
Bracket, submachine gun carrier...	1	Front fender, right side
Guard, front safety	1	Attached to frame
Guard, rear safety	1	Attached to frame
Windshield, cpt	1	On handle bar
Leg shields, cpt (right and left)...	2	Attached to frame

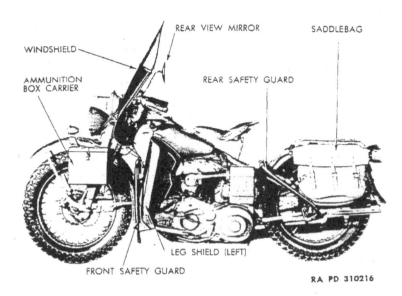

Figure 12—Vehicle Equipment, Left Side

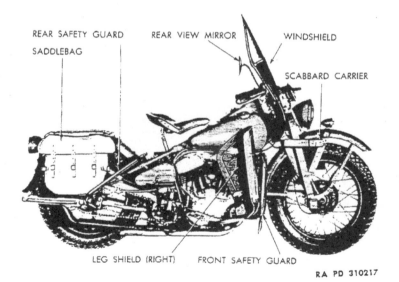

Figure 13—Vehicle Equipment, Right Side

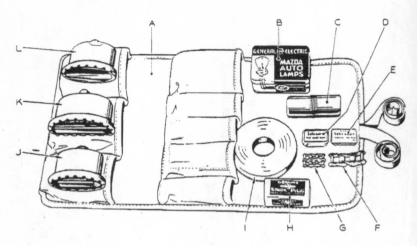

RA PD 310209

Figure 14—Vehicle Spare Parts

23. VEHICLE SPARE PARTS (fig. 14).

† a. Spare Parts.

Item		Number Carried	Where Carried
A	Roll, parts kit	1	In saddlebag
H	Plug, spark (and gasket)	1	In kit roll
F	Link, rear chain repair	1	In kit roll
G	Link, front chain repair	1	In kit roll
K	Lamp-unit, tail blackout	1	In kit roll
J	Lamp-unit, stop blackout	1	In kit roll
L	Lamp-unit, tail and stop	1	In kit roll
B	Lamp bulb kit, head lamps, 5 bulbs	1	In kit roll
C	Kit, tire repair	1	In kit roll
I	Tape, friction	1	In kit roll
D	Caps, tire valve (5 in box)	1	In kit roll
E	Cores, tire valve (5 in box)	1	In kit roll

†EXCEPTION: *No spare parts kit supplied with earlier models. Rear chain repair link only spare part furnished.*

Section VII

MAINTENANCE ALLOCATION

24. SCOPE.

a. The scope of maintenance and repair by the crew and other units of the using arms is determined by the availability of suitable tools, availability of necessary parts, capabilities of the mechanics, time available, and the tactical situation. All of these are variable and no exact system of procedure can be prescribed.

25. ALLOCATION OF MAINTENANCE.

a. Indicated below are the maintenance duties for which tools and parts have been provided for the using arm and maintenance personnel. Replacements and repairs which are the responsibility of ordnance maintenance personnel may be performed by using arm personnel when circumstances permit, within the discretion of the commander concerned. Echelons and words as used in this list of maintenance allocations are defined as follows:

FIRST AND
SECOND ECHELON:
Table III
AR 850-15

Operating organization driver, operator or crew, companies and detachments, battalions, squadrons, regiments, and separate companies and detachments (first and second echelons, respectively).

THIRD ECHELON:
Table III
AR 850-15

Technical light and medium maintenance units, including post and port shops.

FOURTH ECHELON:
Table III
AR 850-15

Technical heavy maintenance and field depot units including designated post and service command shops.

FIFTH ECHELON:
Table III
AR 850-15

Technical base units.

SERVICE:
(Including preventive
maintenance) par. 24 a
(2) and (3) in part
AR 850-15

Checking and replenishing fuel, oil, grease, water and antifreeze, air, and battery liquid; checking and tightening nuts and bolts; cleaning.

REPLACE:
Par. 24 a (5)
AR 850-15

To remove an unserviceable part. assembly, or subassembly from a vehicle and replace it with a serviceable one.

REPAIR:
Par. 24 a (6) in part
AR 850-15

To restore to a serviceable condition. such parts, assemblies or subassemblies as can be accomplished without completely disassembling the assembly or subassembly, and where heavy riveting. or precision machining, fitting, balancing, or alining is not required.

REBUILD:
Par. 24 a (6)
AR 850-15

Consists of stripping and completely reconditioning and replacing in serviceable condition any vehicle or unserviceable part, subassembly, or assembly of the vehicle, including welding. riveting, machining, fitting. alining, balancing. assembling. and testing.

RECLAMATION:
AR 850-15
Par. 4 (c) in part CIR.
75, dated 16 March '43

Salvage of serviceable or economically repairable units and parts removed from vehicles, and their return to stock. This includes the process which recovers and/or reclaims unusable articles or component parts thereof and places them in a serviceable condition.

NOTES: (1) Operations allocated will normally be performed in the echelon indicated by X.
(2) Operations allocated to the third echelon as indicated by E may be performed by these units in emergencies only.
(3) Operations allocated to the fourth echelon by E are normally fifth echelon operations. They will not be performed by the fourth echelon. unless the unit is expressly authorized to do so by the chief of the service concerned.

ECHELONS

CLUTCH	2nd	3rd	4th	5th
Bearings, clutch release—replace	X			
Clutch—replace and/or repair (reline)		X		
Hub, clutch—replace		X		
Hub. clutch—repair			X	
Sprocket assembly, clutch—replace		X		
Sprocket assembly, clutch—repair			X	

CONTROLS AND LINKAGE

	2nd	3rd
Controls and linkage—service and/or replace	X	
Controls and linkage—repair		X

	ECHELONS			
ELECTRICAL GROUP	2nd	3rd	4th	5th
Battery—service (recharge) and/or replace	X			
Battery—repair		X		
Battery—rebuild			E	X
Cables, battery—replace and/or repair	X			
Coil, ignition—replace	X			
Head, speedometer—replace	X			
Head, speedometer—repair		X		
Head, speedometer—rebuild			X	
Horn assembly—replace	X			
Horn assembly—repair		X		
Light assemblies—service and/or replace	X			
Light assemblies—repair		X		
Panel, instrument—replace	X			
Panel, instrument—repair		X		
Switch assemblies—replace	X			
Switch assemblies—repair		X		
Wiring—replace	X			

ENGINE
(V-45"-TWIN ENGINE)

	2nd	3rd	4th	5th
Bearings, main—replace			E	X
Bearings, connecting rod—replace			E	X
Breaker assembly, circuit—replace	X			
Breaker assembly, circuit—repair		X		
Breaker assembly, circuit—rebuild			X	
Carburetor—replace	X			
Carburetor—repair		X		
Carburetor—rebuild			X	
Cleaner, air—service and/or replace	X			
Cleaner, air—repair		X		
Cleaner, air—rebuild			X	
Cylinder assembly—replace		X		
Cylinder assembly—repair			X	
Cylinder assembly—rebuild (recondition)			E	X
Condenser—replace	X			
*Engine assembly—replace	*	X		

*The second echelon is authorized to remove and reinstall items marked by an asterisk. However, when it is necessary to replace an item marked by an asterisk with a new or rebuilt part, subassembly or unit assembly, the assembly marked by an asterisk may be removed from the vehicle by the second echelon *only after* authority has been obtained from a higher echelon of maintenance.

	ECHELONS			
ENGINE (V-45″-TWIN ENGINE) (Cont'd)	2nd	3rd	4th	5th
Engine assembly—repair		X		
Engine assembly—rebuild			E	X
Gasket, cylinder head—replace	X			
Gears, timing—replace		E	X	
Generator assembly—replace	X			
Generator assembly—repair		X		
Generator assembly—rebuild			X	
Head, cylinder—replace and/or repair		X		
Lines and connections—replace	X			
Lines and connections—repair		X		
Pistons, rings and pins assembly—replace		E	E	X
Plug, spark—replace	X			
Points, circuit breaker—service and/or replace	X			
Pump assembly, feed—replace	X			
Pump assembly, feed—repair		X		
Pump assembly, feed—rebuild			X	
Pump assembly, oil—replace	X			
Pump assembly, oil—repair		X		
Pump assembly, oil—rebuild			X	
Pump assembly, oil scavenger—replace and/or repair		X		
Pump assembly, oil scavenger—rebuild			X	
Rod, connecting—replace and/or rebuild (recondition)			X	X
Sprocket, engine—replace	X			
Strained gasoline—replace and/or repair		X		
Valves—service	X			

EXHAUST GROUP

Muffler and exhaust pipe—replace	X			
Muffler and exhaust pipe—repair		X		

MISCELLANEOUS

Bars, safety—replace	X			
Bars, safety—repair		X		
Boxes, ammunition, battery and tool—replace	X			
Boxes, ammunition, battery and tool—repair		X		
Carriers, luggage and scabbard—replace	X			
Carriers, luggage and scabbard—repair		X		
Frame—replace and/or rebuild			E	X
Guards, mud—replace	X			

	ECHELONS			
MISCELLANEOUS (Cont'd)	2nd	3rd	4th	5th
Guards, mud—repair		X		
Plate, skid—replace	X			
Plate, skid—repair		X		
Saddle—replace	X			
Saddle—repair		X		
Saddle—rebuild			X	
Springs, saddle post—replace	X			
Tank, fuel—replace	X			
Tank, fuel—repair		X		
Tank, oil—replace	X			
Tank, oil—repair		X		

SUSPENSION (FRONT)

Bars, handle—replace	X			
Bars, handle—repair		X		
Damper, steering—replace	X			
Drum, brake—replace		X		
Fork, front assembly—replace	X			
Fork, front assembly—repair		X		
Fork, front assembly—rebuild			X	
Fork, spring—replace	X			
Fork, spring—repair		X		
Fork, spring—rebuild			X	
Plate, rocker—replace	X			
Plate, rocker—repair		X		
Shoe assembly, brake—service and/or replace	X			
Shoe assembly, brake—repair (reline)		X		
Springs, cushion and rebound—replace	X			

SUSPENSION (REAR)

Chains, all—replace and/or repair	X			
Drum, brake, rear—replace		X		
Guards, chains—replace	X			
Guards, chains—repair		X		
Shoe assemblies, brake—service and/or replace	X			
Shoe assemblies, brake—repair (reline)		X		
Sprocket, rear—replace		X		
Wheels—replace	X			
Wheels—repair		X		
Wheels—rebuild			E	X

	ECHELONS			
TIRES	2nd	3rd	4th	5th
Casings and tubes—replace	X			
Casings—repair			E	X
Tubes, inner—repair	X			

TRANSMISSION

	2nd	3rd	4th	5th
Spring, kick starter—replace	X			
Sprocket, transmission countershaft—replace	X			
Starter, kick—replace	X			
Starter, kick—repair		X		
*Transmission—replace	*	X		
Transmission—repair		X		
Transmission—rebuild			E	X

VEHICLE ASSEMBLY

	2nd	3rd	4th	5th
Motorcycle—service	X			
Motorcycle—rebuild (with serviceable unit assemblies)			X	E

*The second echelon is authorized to remove and reinstall items marked by an asterisk. However, when it is necessary to replace an item marked by an asterisk with a new or rebuilt part, subassembly or unit assembly, the assembly marked by an asterisk may be removed from the vehicle by the second echelon *only after authority has been obtained from a higher echelon of maintenance.*

Section VIII

SECOND ECHELON PREVENTIVE MAINTENANCE

26. SECOND ECHELON PREVENTIVE MAINTENANCE SERVICES.

a. Regular scheduled maintenance inspections and services are a preventive maintenance function of the using arms, and are the responsibility of commanders of operating organizations.

(1) FREQUENCY. The frequencies of the preventive maintenance services outlined herein are considered a minimum requirement for normal operation of vehicles. Under unusual operating conditions such as extreme temperatures, and dusty or sandy terrain, it may be necessary to perform certain maintenance services more frequently.

(2) FIRST ECHELON PARTICIPATION. The drivers should accompany their vehicles and assist the mechanics while periodic second echelon preventive maintenance services are performed. Ordinarily the driver should present the vehicle for a scheduled preventive maintenance service in a reasonably clean condition; that is, it should be dry, and not caked with mud or grease to such an extent that inspection and servicing will be seriously hampered. However, the vehicle should not be washed or wiped thoroughly clean, since certain types of defects, such as cracks, leaks, and loose or shifted parts or assemblies are more evident if the surfaces are slightly soiled or dusty.

(3) If instructions other than those contained in the general procedures in paragraph (4) or the specific procedures in paragraph (5) which follow, are required for the correct performance of a preventive maintenance service, or for correction of a deficiency, other sections of the vehicle operator's manual pertaining to the item involved, or a designated individual in authority, should be consulted.

(4) GENERAL PROCEDURES. These general procedures are basic instructions which are to be followed when performing the services on the items listed in the specific procedures. The second echelon personnel must be thoroughly trained in these procedures so that they will apply them automatically.

(a) When new or overhauled subassemblies are installed to correct deficiencies, care should be taken to see that they are clean, correctly installed, properly lubricated, and adjusted.

(b) When installing new lubricant retainer seals, a coating of the lubricant should be wiped over the sealing surface of the lip of the seal.

(c) The general inspection of each item applies also to any supporting member or connection, and usually includes a check to see whether the item is in good condition, correctly assembled. secure. or excessively worn. The mechanics must be thoroughly trained in the following explanations of these terms:

1. The inspection for "good condition" is usually an external visual inspection to determine whether or not the unit is damaged beyond safe or serviceable limits. The term "good condition" is explained further by the following: not bent or twisted. not chafed or burned. not broken or cracked, not bare or frayed, not dented or collapsed, not torn or cut.

2. The inspection of a unit to see that it is "correctly assembled" is usually an external visual inspection to see whether or not it is in its normal assembled position in the vehicle.

3. The inspection of a unit to determine if it is "secure" is usually an external visual examination, a hand-feel. or a pry-bar check for looseness; such an inspection should include any brackets. lock washers, lock nuts, locking wires, or cotter pins used in assembly.

4. "Excessively worn" will be understood to mean worn. close to or beyond serviceable limits, and likely to result in a failure if not replaced before the next scheduled inspection.

(d) Special Services. These are indicated by repeating the item numbers in the columns which show the interval at which the services are to be performed, and show that the parts, or assemblies, are to receive certain mandatory services. For example. an item number in one or both columns opposite a *Tighten* procedure. means that the actual tightening of the object must be performed. The special services include:

1. Adjust. Make all necessary adjustments in accordance with the pertinent section of the vehicle operator's manual, special bulletins, or other current directives.

2. Clean. Clean units of the vehicle with dry-cleaning solvent to remove excess lubricant. dirt. and other foreign material. After the parts are cleaned, rinse them in clean dry-cleaning solvent. and dry them thoroughly. Take care to keep the parts clean until reassembled, and be certain to keep dry-cleaning solvent away from rubber or other material which it will damage. Clean the protective grease coating from new parts. since this material is not a good lubricant.

3. Special lubrication. This applies both to lubrication operations that do not appear on the vehicle Lubrication Guide, and to items that do appear on such guides. but should be performed in connection with the maintenance operations. if parts have to be disassembled for inspection or service.

4. Serve. This usually consists of performing special operations. such as replenishing battery water, and draining and refilling units with oil.

5. *Tighten.* All tightening operations should be performed with sufficient wrench-torque (force on the wrench handle) to tighten the unit according to good mechanical practice. Use torque-indicating wrench where specified. Do not overtighten, as this may strip threads, or cause distortion. Tightening will always be understood to include the correct installation of lock washers, lock nuts, and cotter pins provided to secure the tightening.

(e) When conditions make it difficult to perform the complete preventive maintenance procedures at one time, these can sometimes be handled in sections, planning to complete all operations within the week if possible. All available time at halts and in bivouac areas must be utilized, if necessary, to assure that maintenance operations are completed. When limited by the tactical situation, items with special services in the columns should be given first consideration.

(f) The numbers of the preventive maintenance procedures that follow are identical with those outlined on W.D. AGO Form No. 463, which is the Preventive Maintenance Service Work Sheet for Motorcycles. Certain items on the work sheet that do not apply to this vehicle are not included in the procedures in this manual. In general, the numerical sequence of items on the work sheet is followed in the manual procedures, but in some instances there is deviation for conservation of the mechanic's time and effort.

(5) SPECIFIC PROCEDURES. The procedures for performing each item in the 1,000-mile maintenance procedures are described in the following chart. Each page of the chart has a column at its left edge corresponding to the 1,000-mile maintenance.

ROAD TEST

1000 Mile Maintenance	NOTE: If tactical situation does not permit a full road test, perform items 2, 3, 4, 5, 6, 7, 8, 9, 12, and 14, which require slight or no movement of the vehicle. When a road test is possible, it should be for preferably 5, and not over 10 miles.
1	Before-operation Inspection. Perform Before-operation Service listed on W.D. Form No. 418, "Driver's Trip Ticket and Preventive Maintenance Service Record" (described in par. 15), to determine if vehicle is in a satisfactory condition to make the road test safely.
2	Ease of Starting. Start engine and observe action of starter. Note if engine responds readily.
3	Oil Circulation. Oil circulation is normally indicated, by oil signal light (red light) in instrument panel being out. When red light is on, oil is not circulating. Observe for

excess smoke in exhaust. CAUTION: *If red light fails to go out after engine has been started, stop engine at once. Refer to paragraph 30 for possible causes.*

4   **Instruments.** Observe instruments for proper or normal indication and functioning of system to which they apply.

SPEEDOMETER AND ODOMETER. Speedometer must indicate vehicle speed without excessive noise or fluctuation; odometer must record trip and total mileage.

OIL PRESSURE SIGNAL LIGHT. Note whether oil signal light (red light) indicates correctly. After ignition switch is turned on, and before starting engine, the red light should go on, indicating no oil circulation. When engine is started, light should go out.

GENERATOR SIGNAL LIGHT. With switch on. and before starting engine, the green signal light should go on, indicating discharge of battery. After starting engine, increase engine speed to a medium fast idle; green signal light should then go out, indicating generator is charging battery. CAUTION: *Continue observation of signal lights during road test, and if lights should fail to operate as indicated above, stop engine, investigate cause, and correct or report trouble to proper authority.*

5   **Brake Operation.** Test foot brake for safe stop within reasonable distance. Note squeaks or chatter that might indicate wet, oily, dirty, or loose lining, damaged drum, or improper adjustment. Apply hand-operated front brake only in conjunction with rear brake and observe whether it operates effectively in assisting to make a quicker stop.

6   **Clutch Operation.** Before moving vehicle, make sure that clutch pedal has satisfactory free travel before it begins to disengage clutch; that it releases clutch completely before reaching end of travel; and that there are no unusual noises in clutch-release mechanism. When starting vehicle, observe whether clutch grabs, chatters, or slips when fully engaged.

7   **Gearshift.** Shift through entire gear range of transmission and observe whether mechanism operates freely without clashing or jumping out of gear. Note any unusual vibration that might indicate loose engine or transmission mountings.

8   **Unusual Noises.** During entire road test. listen for unusual noises that might indicate worn, loose, damaged, or insufficiently lubricated parts in the entire motorcycle, particularly in engine and accessories, or in the power train.

1000 Mile Maintenance

CAUTION: *Loose primary (front) drive chain, with slack in excess of ½ inch total up-and-down motion, can cause excessive noise which sounds like engine knock. Remove inspection cover for examination of chain.*

9   **Steering.** Observe steering mechanism for indication of looseness or excessive binding through full turning range. With hands resting lightly on handle bars and vehicle in vertical position, observe whether there is any tendency to pull to one side when operating at a reasonable speed. Note any indication of steering instability at higher speeds.

10   **Balance.** If vehicle does not balance properly in operation. inspect for misalinement of rear wheel.

11   **Speedometer and Odometer.** Inspect speedometer for proper operation, excessive fluctuation, or unusual noise. Observe odometer for correct recording of trip and total mileage.

12   **Throttle and Spark Controls.** Set throttle stop screw and low speed needle adjustment so that engine will operate smoothly and will not stall at idling speed. With vehicle running at a speed of 30 miles per hour, or faster, in high gear, turn throttle control grip to "OPEN" and "CLOSED" positions and note whether engine responds instantly to throttle changes. Turn spark control grip and note whether it fully advances and retards ignition timer.

13   **Power and Operation.** Observe engine for normal pulling power, and good operating characteristics in each speed, from first to high gear. Also observe whether engine misses, stalls, knocks excessively, or makes any other unusual noise.

14   **Carburetor Adjustment.** No carburetor adjustment, other than idle adjustment as performed in item 12, is required on this vehicle.

15   **Brake Drum and Hub Temperature.** Immediately after completing road test, feel front and rear brake drums and wheel hubs for overheating.

16   **Power Train Temperatures.** Feel transmission for overheating.

MAINTENANCE OPERATION

17   **Compression Test.** With throttle wide-open, test compression with starter. If engine lacks compression, inspect for leaks.

18   **Transmission.** Inspect transmission for good condition, secure mounting, and leaks. Inspect oil level. Drain and refill

1000 Mile Maintenance

transmission to level of transmission filler plug opening with specified grade of engine oil. CAUTION: *Always drain transmission immediately after it has been warmed and agitated by operation of engine. Refill as soon as draining is completed to avoid hazard of operating without lubricant. Tighten all mounting and assembly bolts securely.*

20   Engine Oil. Inspect oil tank for oil level: drain and refill tank. CAUTION: *Fill to within 1 inch of filler opening and filler cap with specified weight of oil. Always drain immediately after engine operation and refill as soon as draining is completed, to avoid hazard of operating without lubricant.*

21   Battery and Carrier. Clean top of battery. See that battery and carrier are in good condition. and that carrier is securely mounted. Remove cell caps: make sure that vents are open. Test specific gravity with hydrometer and record readings on work sheet. W.D. AGO Form No. 463. Readings below 1.225 indicate need for recharge. or battery failure. Variation between cells of more than 0.025 must be reported. Read and record voltage of battery (6-volt reading is normal). Bring electrolyte to $\frac{9}{16}$ inch above tops of plates, using clean, drinkable water. If excessive looseness of battery in case is noted, check for presence of rubber pad in bottom of case, and make sure rubber pad is installed on top of battery, when battery service is completed.

22   Battery Wires and Terminals. Inspect battery for good condition and secure connections. Look for worn spots in wire insulation. Oil the felt washers on battery terminals.

23   Electrical Wiring. Inspect all electric wiring to see that it is in good condition, securely attached, and connected. Look for worn spots in insulation.

24   Generator Drive and Mounting, and Relay. Inspect generator for secure mounting. After removing left footboard assembly, remove generator and cover. Examine commutator for cleanliness, good condition. or excessive wear. If commutator is dirty, it must be cleaned with No. 00 sandpaper. Blow out with compressed air. If commutator is in bad condition or excessively worn, replace generator. Remove relay cover. being careful to avoid damage to mechanism, and inspect for cleanliness. Blow out with air if wet or dirty. CAUTION: *Do not attempt to adjust relay, or to clean it in any other manner.*

25   Timer (Circuit Breaker). Clean and remove timer cover. See that wiring leads are securely connected and that in-

side of the timer is clean. Inspect breaker points to see that they are clean, well-lined, engaging squarely, and are not excessively pitted, burned, or worn. See that condenser mounting screw is tight. Breaker lever should be free on its pivot and well insulated from the pivot pin. Determine if breaker arm spring exerts normal force against arm. Examine camshaft by hand-feel to see whether it is excessively worn in its bushings; if camshaft bushings are worn excessively, install new timer. If points are slightly burned or pitted, dress them with a fine file. If breaker points are unserviceable, install a new set, taking care to aline them and to adjust gap to 0.022 inch. Apply one drop of oil to breaker arm pivot pin. Use clean cloth to wipe cam and then coat with a very light film of light grease. CAUTION: *Be careful to avoid getting oil or grease on breaker points.*

26 **Spark Plugs.** Remove spark plugs, clean with sandblast cleaner, and inspect for cracked insulators; inspect electrodes for good condition and adjust gap to 0.025 to 0.030 inch.; replace faulty plugs. Be sure to install new gasket with new plug. Inspect radio suppressors on plug cables for good condition and secure attachment.

27 **Ignition and Light Switch.** Make sure that the switch is in good condition and operating properly in all positions.

28 **Lights, Service and Blackout.** See that all lights are clean, in good condition, properly aimed, and securely mounted. Tactical situation permitting, turn switch to each of its positions and observe whether service and blackout lights operate properly, and whether they go out when switched off. Operate dimmer switch on left handle bar to see whether it depresses beam of service headlight. Apply foot brake for check of both blackout and service stop light operation. Inspect lenses for breakage, and headlight reflector for discoloration. Clean all lenses.

29 **Horn.** Tactical situation permitting, sound horn to test for normal signal. Examine horn for good condition, secure mounting, and tight wiring connections.

30 **Cylinder Heads.** If cylinder head gaskets show signs of leakage, tighten head bolts; if leakage persists, new gaskets should be installed. A head bolt wrench (Fed. Stock No. 41-W-1525) is available with which head bolts can be tightened without removing tanks for wrench clearance. If tanks are removed to permit taking off heads and install-

ing new gaskets, bolts should then be tightened evenly with a torque wrench to a tension of 60 foot-pounds minimum. or 65 foot-pounds maximum, when engine is cold.

31   **Cylinder Hold-down Nuts.** If these nuts are loose, or there is excessive oil leakage around cylinder bases, tighten nuts evenly when engine is cold. If excessive leakage persists, new gaskets should be installed. CAUTION: *If cylinder base nuts are loose, perform item 36 before starting engine.*

32   **Engine Mountings.** Inspect top engine mounting bracket and bolt for good condition and security. CAUTION: *Tight seating of the engine bracket mounting bolt is a necessity for effective radio bonding. Inspect four lower engine mounting bolts for signs of looseness. Tighten as required.*

33   **Engine Crankcase.** Examine engine crankcase for good condition and for leaks. Make sure timing gear cover screws, and oil feed and scavenger pump nuts, are tight.

34   **Intake Manifold.** Examine manifold for good condition and secure mounting. Make sure manifold nuts are tight.

35   **Muffler and Exhaust Pipes.** Inspect muffler and exhaust pipes for good condition, secure mounting, and for leaks. Be sure tail pipe opening is not restricted.

36   **Valve Mechanism.** When engine is cold, adjust valve tappet clearance to 0.004-inch minimum, 0.005-inch maximum on intake valve; 0.006-inch minimum, 0.007-inch maximum on exhaust valve. See that valve springs are in good condition and properly secured; that valve tappet adjusting screws and lock nuts are in good condition; and that valve covers are in good condition, secure, and not leaking oil.

37   **Starter.** Examine pedal, crank, and return spring for good condition, correct assembly, and secure mounting. Starter should operate without binding, and return spring should bring starter crank to its disengaged position when foot pressure is removed. CAUTION: *Make sure that starter crank pinch bolt is installed with head of bolt toward rear of vehicle when crank is in upright position.*

38   **Engine Cooling Fins.** Inspect engine cooling fins for good condition and cleanliness. Remove all dirt or foreign matter. Do not apply paint to cooling fins.

39   **Filler Caps and Vents.** Wipe dirt and dust from filler caps of fuel and oil tanks. Inspect caps and gaskets to see that they are in good condition. Note whether vent in fuel filler

1000
Mile
Maintenance cap is open. Reinstall caps, observing that each locks properly on filler neck. Do not interchange fuel and oil tank filler caps.

+0 **Fuel Tank Valves and Lines.** See that valves and lines are in good condition, secure, and not leaking. Test fuel shut-off valve for ample friction to hold valve in reserve position. See that valve lifts freely enough to operate satisfactorily.

+1 **Oil System Leaks.** Examine oil tank, oil lines, vent line, and connections for good condition, secure attachment, and for leaks.

+2 **Carburetor and Fuel Filter (Gasoline Strainer).** Examine carburetor and fuel filter for good condition, secure connections, and for leaks. Shut off fuel tank valve and remove filter (strainer) cap and screen. Wash cap and screen in dry-cleaning solvent, and open shut-off valve slightly to flush filter body. Reassemble screen, gaskets, and cap, being careful not to damage gaskets. Use new gaskets if necessary. Drain water and foreign matter from carburetor bowl by removing bowl drain plug. Open shut-off valve slightly to flush carburetor bowl while plug is out. Replace plug, being careful to avoid crossing threads. Open fuel tank shut-off valve and check for leaks.

+3 **Air Cleaner.** Remove oil cup; inspect condition of oil, and amount of sediment. If service is required, remove filter elements, clean and fill cup to NORMAL level. Wash elements in dry-cleaning solvent, dry thoroughly with compressed air, immerse each element in oil in cup, and reassemble elements and oil cup to air cleaner body immediately. Make sure gaskets are in good condition. NOTE: *Early type round cleaner does not have removable filter element; therefore, the complete cleaner body must be removed to wash element.*

+4 **Gearshift Lever and Linkage.** See that gearshift lever and linkage are in good condition, secure, and not excessively worn. Lubricate all joints with a few drops of engine oil. Adjust shifter lever so that when moved to any gear position in shifter guide on tank, the transmission is shifted to full engagement in corresponding gear.

+5 **Primary Drive.** Remove inspection hole cover from front chain guard. With clutch engaged and transmission in neutral, rotate primary chain to position of least slack. Check chain for ½-inch deflection. Deflection measurement should be total up-and-down free movement. Inspect chain for adequate lubrication. Loosen front and rear chain oiler adjusting screws two turns each. Do not remove screws. Idle engine 1 minute, then tighten screws firmly, but do not force. This operation serves to flush control valves and rear chain oiler pipe.

46   Clutch Pedal and Linkage. Inspect clutch pedal clevis connections and cable to see that they are in good condition and not excessively worn. Check free travel of clutch pedal to make sure it is within specified limits. With foot pedal in fully disengaged position (heel against footboard) clutch release lever must clear sprocket cover stud and nut by about 1_{16} inch; with foot pedal in fully engaged position, clutch release lever must have between $\frac{1}{8}$- and $\frac{1}{4}$-inch free movement on end of foot pedal cable. Lubricate all joints with a few drops of engine oil, including cable at each end of cable housing.

47   Rear Chain and Guard. Inspect rear chain guard for good condition and secure mounting. Remove chain, wash thoroughly in dry-cleaning solvent, and hang it up to dry. See that chain is in good condition, not excessively worn, and has no broken rollers on side plates. Soak chain in SAE 10 engine oil for a short period of time to allow oil to penetrate into all rollers; drain chain, and wipe off excess oil. Inspect countershaft sprocket, and rear wheel sprocket to see that they are in good condition, not excessively worn, and that rear sprocket rivets are tight. Do not reinstall chain until item 71 has been performed. When reinstalling chain, make sure that connecting link is in good condition and securely locked. See that open end of connecting link spring clip is trailing in direction of chain travel. Adjust chain (paragraph 60).

48   Final Drive Sprockets. Inspection of final drive sprockets is made when performing item 47.

50   Paint and Markings. Examine vehicle for good condition and see that paint is not rubbed to a polish, and has no bare spots that might rust or reflect light. See that vehicle markings are legible.

51   Frame. Examine frame for good condition; observe whether it seems to be sprung out of alinement.

52   Steering Head and Fork Stem. Raise front end of vehicle by placing blocks under skid plate. Complete all following items to and including item 71, before lowering vehicle to ground. Examine steering head and fork stems for good

1000 Mile Maintenance condition. Note whether there is up-and-down play caused by loose bearings. Move handle bars through complete range and observe if there is any binding which might indicate improperly adjusted or defective bearings.

53   **Handle Bars.** Examine handle bars for good condition and secure mounting.

54   **Throttle Control.** See that grip is in good condition, that throttle opens and closes completely as grip is turned to its extreme positions, and that control wire and housing are in good condition and secure. Lubricate lightly through hole in rear of grip to avoid rusting and "freezing." If grip does not rotate freely, disassemble grip, clean, and lubricate spiral control parts.

55   **Spark Control.** See that grip is in good condition, that spark is fully advanced and retarded as the grip is turned to its extreme positions; that the control wire and housing are in good condition and secure. Lubricate lightly through hole in rear of grip to avoid rusting and "freezing." If grip does not rotate freely, disassemble grip, clean, and lubricate spiral control parts.

57   **Rear View Mirror.** Clean rear view mirror and examine for good condition and secure mounting.

58   **Front Fender (Mudguard).** Examine front fender for good condition and secure mounting; see that fender does not scrape tire.

59   **Weapon Carrier.** Inspect weapon carrier for good condition and secure mounting.

60   **Ammunition Box.** See that ammunition box and cover are in good condition and securely attached.

61   **Front Springs.** See that front springs and their mountings are in good condition, correctly assembled, and secure.

62   **Front Forks.** See that front forks are in good condition and securely mounted.

63   **Front Fork Rocker Plates (Rocker Arms).** See that front fork rocket plates are in good condition, secure, and not excessively worn. Tighten rocker plate stud nuts securely.

64   **Front Fork Damper.** Inspect steering damper for good condition and to see that it operates freely. Observe whether friction disks are glazed, coated with grease, or excessively worn.

65   **Front Brake and Control Linkage.** See that control linkage operates freely, that all connections are tight, and that

brake is adjusted so that end of hand lever has ¼ free travel before meeting resistance. Look for any indications of a cracked or excessively worn brake drum: badly worn, loose, or grease-saturated linings. If there are any such indications, remove wheel for closer inspection. Look for badly worn brake side cover bushing, shackle bushings and studs, or brake operating stud bearing. Apply a few drops of engine oil to control cable, especially at control housing oiler at left handle bar, and to pin joints.

66   **Front Wheel Alinement and Spokes.** Examine front wheel spokes for presence, good condition, and tightness. If loose spokes are found, tighten evenly, taking care not to distort rim out-of-round, or to cause run-out. Examine rim for good condition, and spin wheel to see that it has no appreciable run-out.

67   **Front Wheel Bearings.** Inspect wheel to see whether bearings are excessively loose. Wheel should have slight amount of side play at rim. Spin wheel and listen for unusual noises which might indicate dry or defective bearings or races. Observe for excessive grease leak. If wheel is found to need only slight cone readjustment to correct excessive bearing play, remove wheel and make this adjustment (par. 126). If indications are found that hub is otherwise in bad order, replace wheel.

EACH SIXTH 1,000-MILE MAINTENANCE SERVICE. Remove front wheel, axle sleeve and bearing, and, together with wheel hub, clean thoroughly in dry-cleaning solvent. Inspect parts for good condition; inspect brake drum. Inspect lining for good condition and secure attachment, and see that it is neither excessively worn nor soaked with grease. Repack bearings, hub, and axle sleeve with specified lubricant. CAUTION: *Make sure that hands and grease are perfectly clean, and that grease is forced between balls onto the cone.* Reassemble and adjust bearings according to instructions in paragraph 126, taking care to see that wheel is properly alined. If unusual operating conditions, such as fording streams, have indicated probable contamination of lubricant, this service should be performed more frequently.

68   **Front Wheel Axle Nuts.** Tighten axle nuts, making sure that cotter pins are installed. Slot in stabilizer plate must be anchored on extended end of left-front rocker plate stud.

69   **Tires, Front and Rear.** Gage tires and inflate to 18 pounds front, and 20 pounds rear (cold). Make sure that valve stems are in good condition and correctly installed, and that valve caps are present and secure. Examine tires for

1000 Mile Maintenance cuts, bruises, breaks, and blisters; remove imbedded glass, nails, or other foreign matter from tire treads; observe treads for excessive or irregular tire wear. At any inspection when unusual or irregular tire wear becomes evident, interchange front and rear tires.

70 **Rear Wheel Alinement and Spokes.** With vehicle on rear stand, inspect in same manner as front wheel (item 66). If it is necessary to aline wheel in frame, make sure sprockets and chains are in correct alinement.

71 **Rear Wheel Bearings and Seals.** Inspect wheel to see whether bearings are excessively loose (wheel should have a slight amount of play at rim). Spin wheel and listen for unusual noise which might indicate dry or defective bearings. Also observe whether there is excessive grease leak. Test for excessive end play. If wheel is found to have considerable side play at rim, indicating excessively worn bearings, or there is evidence of hub assembly being in bad order otherwise, replace wheel. If wheel must be replaced, inspect brake drum and lining for good condition, as indicated in item 75, before reinstalling wheel. CAUTION: *Make sure that wheel mounting socket screws are tight.*

72 **Rear Wheel Axle Nut.** See that rear wheel axle nut is in good condition and securely tightened.

74 **Rear Fender (Mudguard).** Inspect rear fender for good condition and secure attachment.

75 **Rear Brake and Control Linkage.** See that brake control linkage operates freely, and that all connections are secure. Look for indications of badly worn or grease-saturated linings. If brake operating lever stands considerably ahead of vertical, excessive lining wear is indicated. If grease has worked out between brake drum and brake cover, grease-saturated linings are indicated. In either case the wheel should be removed for closer inspection. Inspect drum for cracks or excessive wear. Make sure wheel mounting socket screws are tight. Examine linkage for loose or worn pin or clevis, and for missing washers or cotter pins. Apply a few drops of engine oil to all linkage joints. Brake pedal should have 1-inch free travel before brake begins to meet resistance. Adjust length of brake rod at brake operating lever to provide 1-inch free pedal travel.

77 **Footboard and Rest.** Examine footboard and rest for good condition and secure attachment.

78 **Saddle Spring and Hinge.** Examine saddle for good condition and secure mounting, paying particular attention to

1000 Mile Maintenance torn leather, ripped seams, sagging or broken spring in seat post, and excessive wear in front hinge. CAUTION: *Make sure that spring wire clip properly locks the saddle rear hinge clevis pin.*

79 Luggage Carrier. Examine luggage carrier for good condition and secure mounting.

80 Saddle Bags. Examine saddle bags for good condition, cleanliness, and secure fastening to luggage carrier. Note particularly whether leather is torn, seams ripped, or straps and buckles missing or damaged.

81 Tools, Tire Pump, and Equipment. Inspect tool kit, tools, tire pump, and other equipment for good condition, cleanliness, serviceability, and proper stowage. Make sure that tire pump is securely clamped to motorcycle frame. Check all items with stowage list (pars. 21, 22 and 23). Make sure that vehicle manuals and Accident Report Form No. 26 are present on vehicle and legible.

82 Safety Guards. Inspect safety guards for good condition and secure mounting.

83 Leg Shields. Inspect leg shields for good condition and secure mounting. NOTE:. *Motorcycles operating in warm weather should not be equipped with leg shields, as they seriously hamper engine cooling.*

84 Skid Plate. Examine skid plate for good condition and secure mounting. CAUTION: *Skid plate must be present.*

85 Vehicle Lubrication. Lubricate all points of vehicle in accordance with instructions in this manual, Lubrication Guide, current lubrication bulletins or directives, and the following instructions:

Any unit that required disassembly for inspection purposes must be lubricated correctly unless the vehicle is to be deadlined for the repair of that unit. Use only clean lubricant. Keep all lubricant containers covered except when used during lubrication. Before applying lubricant, always wipe dirt from the lubrication fitting or plug so that dirt will not enter with the lubricant. If lubricant fittings or plugs are missing or damaged, replace them. Clean the hole in which the fitting is to be installed, and lubricate after the new fitting has been installed.

Lubricant must be applied properly. On unsealed joints or bushings, apply lubricant until it appears at openings. However, lubricate sparingly the front wheel hub, rear wheel hub, front brake side cover bushing, front brake oper-

1000
Mile
Maintenance ating lever stud, and rear brake operating lever stud, to prevent grease reaching brake linings. Rider should be advised whenever wheel bearings are serviced or adjusted, so that during the next road operation he may determine whether bearings or brake drums are running hot, due to overtight adjustment of bearings, or a dragging brake.

Do not apply more than specified amount of lubricant to generator or timer (circuit breaker). To do so may cause failure of the unit.

Wipe off excess applied lubricant that may drip onto brake or operating surfaces, soil clothes, or detract from vehicle's appearance.

Parts or assemblies that have already been lubricated while disassembled for inspection, gear cases that have been drained and refilled as mandatory items in the procedure, and those parts that have been indicated for special lubrication, will be omitted from the general lubrication of the vehicle.

86   **Final Road Test.** Make a final road test, reinspecting items 2 to 16, inclusive. Be sure to recheck transmission to see that lubricant is at correct level and not leaking. Confine this road test to the minimum distance necessary to make satisfactory observation. Correct or report all deficiencies found during final road test to designated authority.

ORGANIZATION TOOLS AND EQUIPMENT

27. TOOLS AND EQUIPMENT.

a. Refer to SNL-N 19 for common hand tools available to second echelon.

b. Refer to list given below for all special tools available to second echelon.

Special Tool Description	Manufacturer's Number	Federal Stock Number
Hydrometer, battery, special	HRD 11831-X	18-H-1242
Tool, repair, drive chain, motorcycle universal	HRD 12039-X	41-T-3320

Tool, spoke tightening,
  special, $\frac{3}{4}$-inch, for
  small diameter spokes ....
	IMC 7-T-3259	41-T-3368-20

Wrench, cyl. base nut, twin.....	HRD 12650-29	2941-W-872-10
Wrench, head bolt	HRD 12047-30A	41-W-1525
Wrench, manifold, 45-in. twin....	HRD 12003-X	41-W-1570-10
Wrench, spark plug	HRD 11929-40	41-W-3334
Wrench, spoke nipple, front wheel	HRD 12032-X	41-W-3339
Wrench, spoke nipple, heavy duty rear wheel.............	HRD 12033-39	41-W-3340
Wrench, tappet and dbl-head open-end $\frac{7}{16}$- and $1\frac{3}{8}$-in.......	HRD 11806-31	41-W-3617

Section X

TROUBLE SHOOTING

28. INTRODUCTION.

a. Trouble shooting for the entire vehicle is given in this section. The engine trouble shooting paragraph traces trouble to a system affecting engine performance: for example, fuel or ignition. To trace trouble to one or more defective components of a system, it is necessary to refer to the pertinent paragraph of this section when the defective system or systems have been located in the engine trouble shooting paragraph.

b. The material given in this section applies to the operation of the vehicle under normal conditions. If extreme conditions of temperature occur, it is assumed the operator of the vehicle has prepared his vehicle for use for the conditions encountered.

29. ENGINE.

a. Instruction. This subparagraph traces troubles to a system affecting engine performance. Step b below gives simple engine tests to determine the mechanical condition of the engine. References in step b refer to step c for engine mechanical troubles, or to pertinent paragraphs in this section for system troubles, or when a test indicates a special unit is faulty, to the pertinent paragraph in this manual.

(1) ENGINE DOES NOT TURN OVER WHEN FOOT STARTER IS OPERATED.

(a) Clutch slipping. Check adjustment (par. 48).

(b) Sheared engine sprocket key. Replace (par. 65).

(c) Starter clutch stuck by congealed oil. Free starter clutch. Use proper grade of oil.

(d) Starter clutch worn. Refer to maintenance personnel.

(e)   Engine locked (seized). Refer to organization mechanic.

(2)   ENGINE TURNS OVER WHEN CRANKED BUT DOES NOT START.

(a)   Fuel supply valve closed. Open valve.

(b)   Empty fuel tank. Fill tank.

(c)   Fuel system faulty. Refer to paragraph 31.

(d)   Ignition system faulty. Refer to paragraph 32.

(e)   Battery weak or dead. Refer to paragraph 34.

(f)   Insufficient compression. Refer to step b, below.

(3)   WEAK COMPRESSION. Refer to step **b** below for test.

(a)   Improper valve tappet adjustment. Adjust (par. 43).

(b)   Valves sticking. Use dry-cleaning solvent to free valve stems in guides.

(c)   Faulty lubrication. Refer to paragraph 20.

(d)   Loose cylinder head bolts and/or faulty gasket. Tighten head bolts or replace gasket (par. 41).

(4)   OVERHEATING.

(a)   Faulty fuel system. Refer to paragraph 31.

(b)   Dirt on cylinders. Clean fins on cylinder, especially the fins on cylinder head.

(c)   Defective lubrication system. Refer to paragraph 30.

(d)   Defective ignition system. Refer to paragraph 32.

(e)   Idling engine without having vehicle in motion. Do not idle engine longer than 1 minute.

(f)   Valve tappet adjustment incorrect. Refer to step **b** (1) below for test, to paragraph 43 for adjustment.

(g)   Drive chains too tight. Adjust (pars. 59 and 60).

(h)   Excessive carbon deposits. Refer to organization mechanic.

(5)   LACK OF POWER.

(a)   Defective fuel system. Refer to paragraph 31.

(b)   Defective ignition system. Refer to paragraph 32.

(c)   Overheating. Refer to step (4) above.

(d)   Defective lubricating system. Refer to paragraph 30.

(e)   Poor compression. Refer to step (3) above.

(f)   Drive chains too tight. Adjust (pars. 59 and 60).

(g)   Brakes dragging. Adjust (pars. 96 and 97).

(6)   POPPING AND SPITTING THROUGH CARBURETOR.

(a)   Water in fuel. Water may be present in fuel tank and carburetor. Drain and refill fuel tank and carburetor bowl.

(b)   Incorrect valve tappet adjustment or sticky valves. Test (step **b** (1) below). Adjust tappets (par. 43).

(c) Defective ignition system. Refer to paragraph 32.

(d) Defective fuel system. Refer to paragraph 31.

(e) Weak and/or broken valve springs. Refer to higher authority.

(7) SPARK KNOCK.

(a) Defective ignition system. Refer to paragraph 32.

(b) Excessive carbon deposits. Refer to step b (2) below.

(c) Defective fuel system. Refer to paragraph 31.

(d) Defective lubrication system. Refer to paragraph 30.

(8) POUNDING AND EXCESSIVE METALLIC NOISE.

(a) Front drive chain too loose. Refer to paragraph 36.

(b) Engine sprocket loose on shaft.

(c) Excessively loose valve tappets. Adjust (par 43).

(d) Engine mounting bolts loose. Tighten.

(e) Transmission mounting stud nuts loose. Tighten (par. 60).

(f) Spark timing incorrect. Adjust.

(g) Internal parts of engine worn or broken. Notify organization mechanic.

b. Tests to Determine Mechanical Condition of Engine.

(1) RINGS AND VALVES. This is a simple compression test. If possible, make this test with the engine warm. Ignition switch must be off. Crank engine slowly, placing entire weight of body on starter crank. Engine compression should sustain the weight of an average size rider several seconds before crank passes through complete range of its travel. If engine offers little resistance to starter crank in testing either or both cylinders, it is an indication that compression is not adequate in one or both cylinders. No clearance or insufficient clearance at valve tappets; valves sticking in guides; valves seating poorly; cylinder heads leaking; spark plugs loose in heads; piston rings badly worn and/or broken; cylinder and pistons badly worn, or lack of lubrication could cause the above condition. Make external checks first: See that oil is in tank, that spark plugs are tight, and examine around cylinder heads for signs of leaking oil deposits. In extremely cold weather, resistance to the starter crank is increased by "stiff" oil in engine and transmission. Therefore, do not mistake this condition to indicate actual engine compression.

(2) ABNORMAL ENGINE NOISE. Owing to constructional design of the motorcycle, correct adjustment of the several units and components is necessary for smooth and normally quiet engine operation. Many motorcycles have been "deadlined" and engines exchanged because simple tune-up service and correct adjustment of components have been neglected. Rough, jerky, and noisy engine action at low speed riding is usually caused by excessively loose front and rear drive chains, or by a transmission being loose in its frame mounting.

Fast idling of engine with the front drive chain too loose, may give the false impression that the engine bearings and pistons need replacement service. Engine sprocket loose on its shaft will cause a pounding noise similar to that of badly worn engine bearings. If front drive chain is too tight, or engine sprocket and chain are badly worn, a grinding noise results, seeming to come from the engine. Excessively loose valve tappets will cause abnormal metallic noise in the valve timing gear train and engine crankcase. Spark advanced too far will cause rough engine performance at low speeds as well as spark knock, pounding, and overheating. Engine pounding and rough operation with consequent noise, result from loose mounting bolts. Generator mounted to give insufficient gear-tooth clearance will cause "howl" in gear case.

30. ENGINE LUBRICATING SYSTEM.

a.   Action of the oil feed pump is indicated by the red signal light located in right side of instrument panel. (Red signal light is normally grounded by the oil pressure switch. When oil pump pressure is built up several pounds, diaphragm opens the signal light circuit.) Action of the scavenger (oil return) pump is indicated (engine running) by oil dripping from $\frac{1}{8}$-inch hole in oil return tube (large tube) inside oil tank, just back of oil gage rod (dip stick) tube. Since the oil feed pump and scavenger pump are separate units, operated individually, it is possible (due to faulty unit) for either to function alone, thus affecting engine oil pressure and return of oil to the tank. Action of the vent pipe (small pipe) located within the oil tank is of a "breather" nature; its function not being indicated in any manner. Before attempting to diagnose trouble in engine lubricating system, rider must be familiar with and understand indications by instrument panel signal lights (par. 7 f).

b.   **Red Signal Light Fails to Burn When Ignition and Light Switch is Turned On.**

(1)   Check other lights to determine if battery is "up" and that switch and wiring connections between battery and switch are in good order. See that wire connection is secure and screw is tight on oil pressure switch terminal. Failure of light to burn after these checks indicates that either the lamp is burned out or oil pressure switch is faulty.

(2)   Test to eliminate the oil pressure switch by removing wire from switch terminal; ground wire on switch body and note if red light burns with ignition and light switch in "ON" position. If light burns, it indicates that oil pressure switch is faulty, and must be replaced. If light does not burn in making this test, it indicates that lamp is burned out. Remove panel cover (par. 119) and replace lamp.

c. **Red Signal Light Continues to Burn After Engine Is Operated Above Idling Speeds**

(1)   Check oil supply in tank. If light fails to go out after engine is warm, or after 1 minute of operation, further checks must be made to locate trouble, as indication points to faulty engine lubrication system, or fault in signal circuit. Eliminate the signal system first.

(2)   Test oil pressure signal switch to panel signal light circuit. Remove wire from oil pressure switch terminal by turning on ignition and light switch and observing red signal light. If light burns, short circuit in wiring exists. If light does not burn, it indicates normal condition, leaving oil pressure switch of the signal circuit tq be tested.

(3)   Install new oil pressure switch and start engine. If red signal light goes out after engine is operated above idling speeds, it indicates trouble in oil pressure signal switch. If red signal light continues to burn, it indicates trouble in oil feed pump. Replace pump (par. 44).

d.   **Excessive Smoke Issues from Exhaust and Oil Spray Issues from Gear Case Breather Outlet.** This is an indication that the scavenger pump is not draining engine crankcase and returning oil to tank. With engine running at idle speed, examine oil return in tank. Remove tank oil cap, and with a small flashlight (tactical situation permitting), observe whether or not oil is dripping from $\frac{1}{8}$-inch hole in oil return tube. Hole is on under side of tube and is located just back of oil gage rod tube. If observation is poor, place finger over hole and feel for pulsation of oil pressure. If oil does not return to tank, scavenger pump is faulty. Should the crankcase breather valve be incorrectly timed, smoke will issue from the exhaust, but not as noticeably as when scavenger pump is not working. Refer to step e below for this condition.

e.   **Smoke Issues from Exhaust and Excessive Oil Condition Exists Around Cylinder Exhaust Ports (where exhaust pipes enter cylinders).** Engine scavenger pump and crankcase breather valve are one unit, operated by worm gear located behind engine shaft pinion gear. Although scavenger pump is not "timed," the breather valve sleeve which drives it must be timed to balance the engine lubricating system. If for any reason the scavenger pump unit is removed from engine base, the breather valve must be retimed (within the gear case) when pump assembly is replaced. Incorrectly timed breather valve will force oil past piston rings, causing some smoke, besides forcing oil out through exhaust ports, causing excessive oily condition around exhaust pipes where they enter cylinder ports.

31. FUEL SYSTEM.

a.   Many symptoms which might be attributed to the air-fuel system are, in reality, due to faulty ignition. Before attempting any but the obviously required adjustments, check the ignition system thoroughly. Gasoline tank supply valve is a dual purpose valve, and its operation is explained in paragraph 5 b.

b.   Shut off gasoline supply valve. Disconnect fuel line at strainer, open valve, and observe free flow of fuel from pipe. If line is plugged, remove, clean out, and replace.

c.   Remove, disassemble, clean, and install fuel strainer (par. 72).

d.   **Hard Starting, Spitting, and Misfiring Caused by Water in Fuel.** Remove drain screw from carburetor bowl, drain bowl, and replace screw. Take care not to cross drain screw threads when replacing. If there is still evidence of water, dirt, or other foreign matter after bowl is drained, replace carburetor (pars. 70 and 71). Remove air cleaner oil cup and inspect for evidence of water in oil. Drain, clean, refill to correct level mark, and replace cup. Should above procedure fail to eliminate trouble, drain fuel tank by removing drain plug located under tank in forward position. Replace drain plug and refill tank with fuel.

e.   **Hard Starting, or Missing at Idling and Low Speeds.** Carburetor low speed circuit in need of adjustment.(par. 68). Carburetor high speed circuit is controlled by a *fixed* jet.

f.   **Impossible to Obtain Satisfactory Carburetor Adjustment; Lean Spot Between Idling and Up to 30 Miles per Hour Speeds.** Carburetors in service for some time become dirty and crust forms in the throttle barrel, making satisfactory low speed adjustment difficult, if not impossible. Replace carburetor (pars. 70 and 71).

g.   **Fuel Leaking from Carburetor.** Evidence of dirt in float valve, incorrect float level, or faulty float. Replace carburetor (pars. 70 and 71).

h.   **Difficult Starting, Fuel Mixture Too Rich.** Air cleaner oil cup overfilled, or cleaner elements exceptionally dirty, choking off adequate air supply to carburetor. Check the oil cup level. If oil cup level is correct, remove, clean, and install cleaner elements (par. 76).

32.   IGNITION SYSTEM.

a.   When checking ignition system for trouble, make the most obvious and simple checks first. For example: Turn on ignition and light switch, observe lights to ascertain battery current supply; then check to see that current is reaching spark coil, circuit breaker, etc. Faulty spark plugs are responsible for the great majority of engine ignition troubles. There is no service for spark plugs other than sandblast cleaning and correct adjustment of electrodes. Questionable spark plugs must be replaced (par. 83).

b.   Remedy all poor connections in ignition wiring system (fig. 48).

c. Remove circuit breaker cover, operate engine with starter pedal, and observe opening and closing of circuit breaker points. Correct point gap when breaker lever fiber is on highest point of cam is 0.022 inch. For adjustment refer to paragraph 84.

d. **Testing for High Tension Spark.** Spark at plug gaps depends upon condition and operation of circuit breaker points, condition of condenser, and condition of spark coil and high-tension cables. Testing the ignition system is best done by means of elimination, testing each unit by replacement until trouble is located; then replacing serviceable units which were removed.

(1) Remove spark plug cable terminal from either plug, leaving other cable and plug connected (to effect ground return of high-tension current); turn engine until circuit breaker points are closed; turn ignition and light switch on; hold high tension cable terminal ¼ inch from cylinder; open and close circuit breaker points with finger and observe spark jump at gap. If spark jumps gap, it indicates ignition primary and secondary circuits are complete.

(2) No spark at high-tension gap calls for testing of primary and secondary circuits. Turn engine until breaker points are held open; hold cable end ¼ inch from cylinder; turn ignition switch on and with the bit of a screwdriver, make a good ground connection between breaker movable (lever) point, and the ground. If a good spark is obtained at high-tension cable terminal gap when ground connection made by screwdriver is broken, clean or replace faulty breaker points (par. 84).

(3) If circuit breaker points are in good condition, but no spark (or a very weak spark) occurs at high-tension gap, replace condenser (par. 85) and repeat test under step (1) above. If replacement of condenser does not remedy trouble, replace spark coil (par. 89).

(4) If tests made under steps d (1), (2), and (3) above show ignition system to be in good order (no units having been replaced), and ignition trouble still exists, it means that breaker points, condenser, and spark coil must be replaced with new units and engine road test made with each replacement until trouble has been located and remedied.

e. **Ignition System Tests Satisfactory but Engine Starts Hard, Overheats or Misses.** Clearly an indication that spark plugs are faulty. Remove spark plugs, clean with sandblast, regap points between 0.028 inch to 0.030 inch and reinstall. Replace defective plugs with new ones of correct (No. 2) heat range (par. 83).

f. **Engine Misses After Warm-up, or When Quite Hot.** Replacement of spark plugs should remedy this trouble. If it does not, then either the condenser or spark coil is at fault. Replace condenser first (par. 85). If new condenser fails to correct trouble, replace spark coil (par. 89).

33.   GENERATING SYSTEM.

a.   **Panel Green Signal Light Continues to Burn Above 20 Miles per Hour.** Correct faulty wiring and connections between battery and generator. Refer to figure 55. Inspect condition of relay and, if necessary, replace (par. 95). Inspect brushes and commutator of generator. Clean commutator if necessary (par. 91). If brushes are sticking in holders or badly worn, replace generator (pars. 93 and 94).

b.   **Generator Output Fails to Keep Battery Charged Although Green Signal Light Behavior Is Satisfactory.** Test battery; if it will not hold charge, or is defective, replace (par. 113). If the machine is used most of the time for night operation, have a higher echelon increase the generating charging rate. Inspect brushes and commutator of generator. Clean commutator if necessary (par. 91). If brushes are badly worn or sticking in holders, replace generator (pars. 93 and 94).

34.   ELECTRICAL SYSTEM.

a.   **Panel Lamps Do Not Light When Switch Is Turned On.** Examine each lamp and if burned out, replace (par. 120). Examine battery; if discharged, replace (par. 113). Remedy defective wiring and connections (fig. 71). Test light switch; if defective, replace (par. 116). Test blackout light switch (in lamp body); if defective, replace lamp (par. 114).

b.   **Lights Burn Dim but Brighten Up Considerably When Engine Is Accelerated.** Test battery with hydrometer. If it is not fully charged, replace (par. 113). Remedy defective wiring, connections, and switches in circuit (fig. 73). If the battery runs down again after a short period of operation, have the generator output increased (refer to a higher echelon).

c.   **Lights Exceed Normal Brilliancy When Accelerating Engine.** Examine battery; if defective, replace (par. 113). Remedy faulty wiring and connections (fig. 73). Do not forget the ground connection of the lamp body.

d.   **Blackout Stop Lamp and/or Service Stop Lamp Fail to Light.** If the unit is burned out, replace it (par. 115). If the brake pedal is not operating switch, remedy the faulty operation. Remedy all faulty wiring and connections (fig. 73).

e.   **Horn Does Not Sound When Ignition and Light Switch Is Turned On and Horn Button Is Pressed.** Test battery by turning on lights. If lights are dim, replace battery (par. 113). Remedy defective wiring and connections (fig. 73). If the horn does not respond to adjustment, replace (par. 117).

35.   TRANSMISSION AND CLUTCH.

a.   Need for attention to clutch and controls is indicated by clutch slipping under load or dragging (transmission gears will shift hard and clash) when in disengaged position. In either case, the first thing to be checked is adjustment of controls: this being the attention usually needed. Indication that gear shifter controls are in need of adjustment is when transmission gears "jump" out of engagement when accelerating vehicle or when under heavy pull. CAUTION: *This warning must not be disregarded.*

(1)   CLUTCH SLIPS WHEN FULLY ENGAGED. Adjust clutch control (par. 48). Adjust clutch spring tension (par. 48). If the clutch still slips, replace either the disks, springs, or both (par. 48).

(2)   CLUTCH DRAGS WHEN FULLY DISENGAGED. Adjust control (par. 48). Adjust spring tension (par. 48).

(3)   CLUTCH RATTLES WHEN IN DISENGAGED POSITION, ENGINE IDLING. In this case, the clutch probably was not properly assembled. Refer to paragraph 51 a.

(4)   TRANSMISSION "JUMPS" OUT OF GEAR UPON ACCELERATING VEHICLE, OR WHEN UNDER HEAVY PULL. Adjust shifter lever control linkage (par. 54).

(5)   TRANSMISSION GEARS SHIFT HARD OR CLASH WHEN CLUTCH IS FULLY DISENGAGED. Adjust clutch control linkage and spring tension (par. 48). Make sure the transmission mounting bolts and units are tight (pars. 57 and 58). Drain and fill transmission with correct lubricant (fig. 10). If the above methods fail to cure the symptom, refer to a higher authority.

36.   WHEELS AND CHAINS.

a.   **Transmission Countershaft and Rear Wheel Sprockets Show Excessive Wear on One Side of Teeth.** Adjust the position of the rear wheel axle to aline the rear wheel sprocket with the transmission sprocket (par. 60). If they cannot be alined, the frame is out of alinement, and the trouble must be referred to a higher authority.

b.   **Chains Produce Grinding Noise with Engine Idling and Vehicle on Rear Stand.** If either chain is adjusted too tight, adjust to proper tension (pars. 59 and 60). Examine both chains for presence of dirt and grit. If dirty, clean and lubricate them (par. 20 c (10)). If either chain is dry, adjust chain oilers (par. 61). Badly worn chains and sprockets will cause this symptom: the worn parts must be replaced (pars. 62 and 63).

c.   **Front Chain Dry and/or Red (Rusty) in Appearance.** The chain in this condition has not been receiving enough lubrication.

Adjust chain oiler (par. 61). If the chain is damaged from lack of oil, replace (par. 62).

d.   **Rough or Jerky Vehicle Operation at Low Speed.** Chains are too loose. Adjust (pars. 59 and 60).

e.   **Excessive Side Play at Rim of Front Wheel.** Adjust bearing cones (par. 126). If the cones and/or hub races are badly worn, replace wheel (par. 125).

f.   **Front Wheel Spinning Test Produces Grinding, Grating Noise (not in brake).** The wheel bearings are defective. Replace wheel (par. 125).

g.   **Rear Wheel Has Excessive Side Play at Rim of Wheel.** The hub bearings are defective. Replace wheel (par. 127).

h.   **Rear Wheel Has Side Play in Excess of 0.010 inch on Axle.** The thrust washers of hub are worn or damaged. Replace wheel (par. 127).

i.   **Rear Wheel Spinning Test Produces Grinding, Grating Noise (chain removed).** Tighten wheel mounting screws. If this does not correct noise, replace wheel (par. 127).

37.   BRAKES.

a.   **Rear Brake Does Not Hold When Foot Pedal Is Depressed.** If the brake linings are wet, operate the vehicle and apply a slight pressure to the brake pedal to dry out linings. After drying the linings adjust brake rod length (par. 96 b). If the brake operating lever stands ahead of the vertical position with brake applied, or the brake does not hold, replace the defective brake shoes (par. 96).

b.   **Rear Brake Squeaks or Chatters When Used.** Tighten side plate sleeve nut, if it is loose. Adjust shoe position (par. 96). If the operating camshaft and/or side cover bearing is worn, replace the assembly (par. 96). If the brake shoe spring is defective, replace (par. 96). If the lining on the brake shoes is loose, worn, or defective, replace shoes (par. 96). If the brake drum is worn or damaged, replace the brake drum and sprocket assembly (par. 96).

c.   **Rear Brake Drags (vehicle on rear stand).** Adjust linkage (par. 96). If it still drags, equalize shoe assemblies, and adjust linkage (par. 96).

d.   **Front Brake Does Not Hold When Hand Lever Is Operated.** Adjust brake control (par. 97). If brakes are wet, operate vehicle a short distance with slight pressure on brake lever to dry out linings. If brake does not hold, replace shoes (par. 97).

e.   **Front Brake Drags.** Adjust control linkage (par. 97). If brake still drags, equalize shoes and readjust control linkage (par. 97).

f.   **Front Brake Action Rough and/or Chatters.** Adjust control linkage assembly (par. 97). If malfunction continues, examine brake

shoes, shoe spring, camshaft bearing and side cover bearing. Replace
any defective parts or assemblies (par. 97).

38. STEERING.

a. **Motorcycle Pulls to One Side.** Inspect and correct alinement
of rear wheel (par. 60). If the front forks are bent or twisted, replace
(par. 98). If trouble persists, refer to higher authority.

b. **Motorcycle Weaves from Side to Side.** Adjust steering
damper to suit speed and road conditions. If this fails, inflate tires
to correct pressure. Make sure rear wheel mounting screws are tight.
If the steering head bearings are too tight, weaving will result. Check
the steering head bearings (par. 98), and adjust if necessary.

c. **Motorcycle Shimmies at High Speed.** Inflate tires to correct
pressure. Adjust steering damper to suit speed and road conditions.
If the tire tread is unevenly worn, and shifting tires does not correct
the condition, replace the defective casings. Make sure the axle nuts
are tight. If the rocker plate studs and bushings are badly worn, or
the fork springs are broken, replace (par. 98).

Section XI

ENGINE

39. DESCRIPTION AND DATA.

a. **Description.** This 2-cylinder, V-type, air-cooled gasoline engine of L-head design operates on the 4-stroke, 4-cycle principle. Flywheel and connecting rod assemblies operate on roller bearings. Engine is fitted with low-expansion aluminum alloy, cam-ground, horizontally slotted pistons and with deep-finned aluminum cylinder heads. As viewed from left side of vehicle (drive chain side), rotation of engine is counterclockwise.

b. Lubrication system is of dry-sump type, in which oil supply is maintained in a tank away from engine. Oil is circulated by a supply feed pump and a scavenger, return pump. This oil circulating system plays a most important part in cooling the engine as well as lubricating it.

c. **Data.**

Type of engine.......2-cylinder, V-type, L-head, air-cooled
Cylinder bore . . . . $2\frac{3}{4}$ in.
Stroke . . . . $3\frac{13}{16}$ in.
Piston displacement . . . . 45.12 cu in.
Compression ratio 5.0:1
Horsepower (N.A.C.C. Rating) 6.05
Engine number (serial), left side of engine base,
    just below front cylinder.

40. TUNE-UP.

a. Tune-up consists of making correct adjustment to valve tappets, circuit breaker ignition points, spark plug electrodes; checking and correcting ignition timing; draining and flushing carburetor bowl; cleaning and flushing gasoline strainer; cleaning muffler outlet, servicing air cleaner, and adjusting carburetor.

(1) Valve tappet adjustment (par. 43).

(2) Circuit breaker point adjustment (par. 84).

(3)   Spark plug service (par. 83).

(4)· Timing ignition (par. 86).

(5)   Draining carburetor bowl (par. 73).

(6)   Cleaning fuel strainer (par. 72).

(7)   Cleaning muffler outlet requires freeing outlet of carbon deposits. caked dirt. oil, etc.. with blade of screwdriver, or other suitable tool. Do not enlarge outlet size when cleaning.

(8)   Servicing air cleaner (par. 76).

(9)   Adjusting carburetor (par. 68).

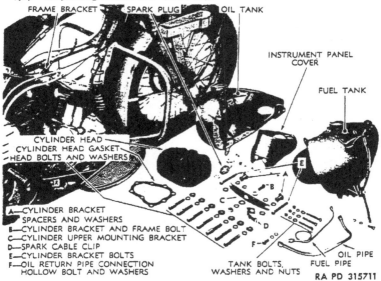

Figure 15—Disassembly for Head Gasket Replacement

41. REPLACEMENT OF HEAD GASKET (fig. 15).

a. **Removal.** Refer to figure 15, illustrating necessary parts and units to be removed to perform this operation.

(1)   Remove instrument panel cover (par. 119).

(2)   Remove gasoline tank and oil tank (par. 107).

(3)   Remove cylinder head bracket to frame lug bolt; this will free clamp which secures front spark plug cable. Pay particular attention to shim washers placed between cylinder head bracket and frame lug, as these washers must be replaced when installing cylinder head.

(4)   Remove spark plug, or plugs.

(5)   Remove cylinder head bolts, using head bolt wrench 41-W-1525. NOTE: *On some 42 WLA models, plain washers (0.095-inch thick), in addition to regular (heavy) cylinder head bolt washers, were used to prevent cylinder head bolts from bottoming.*

(6)   Perform carbon removal (head only). Refer to paragraph 42.

b.   Installing Gasket and Head (fig. 15).

(1)   Clean top of cylinder. Apply a light application of grease or oil to both sides of gasket before locating on cylinder head. Place head on cylinder.

(2)   Install head bolts, using heavy washers (also 0.095-inch thick plain washers, if any were removed). If in doubt as to use of 0.095-inch thick washers in addition to regular washers, measure depth of bolt holes in cylinder head. Head having hole depth of $\frac{31}{32}$ inch must use the 0.095-inch thick washers in addition to regular washers. Head having bolt hole depth of $1\frac{1}{16}$ inch does not require the 0.095-inch thick washers.

(3)   Install cylinder frame bracket with the two long bolts, special (spool-shaped) spacers, and flat washers. The spacers go between cylinder heads and frame bracket. A flat washer goes under the head of each long cylinder bolt, above the bracket; some engines may have flat washers between the spacers and the bracket.

(4)   Tighten head bolts evenly to ensure a tight cylinder head joint. Use head bolt wrench 41-W-1525, first turning down bolts just snug, then tightening each bolt $\frac{1}{8}$ to $\frac{1}{4}$ turn at a time, until all are securely tightened. If torque wrench is available, tighten head bolts to 60 foot-pounds minimum, 65 foot-pounds maximum tension when engine is cold.

42.   CARBON REMOVAL.

a.   At time cylinder head is removed for gasket replacement, carbon must be removed from head only.

43.   VALVE TAPPET ADJUSTMENT (fig. 16).

a.   Adjust Tappets with Engine Cold. Before loosening valve spring covers, a light application of oil around top edge of each cover will facilitate raising cover without damage to seal packing.

(1)   Loosen valve spring covers; use tappet and valve cover wrench 41-W-3617.

(2)   Before checking or adjusting tappet clearance, make sure valve is seated and that tappet is at lowest position, by turning engine ahead until like tappet (inlet or exhaust, whichever one is being

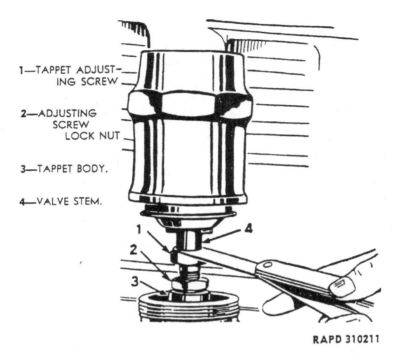

1—TAPPET ADJUST-
   ING SCREW

2—ADJUSTING
   SCREW
   LOCK NUT

3—TAPPET BODY.

4—VALVE STEM.

RAPD 310211

Figure 16—Valve Tappet Adjustment

adjusted) in the other cylinder is at highest position (valve fully open). Inlet valves are located nearest the carburetor manifold.

(4)   Loosen adjusting screw lock nut ("2," fig. 16) slightly before turning adjusting screw (fig. 16).

(5)   Adjust inlet valve tappets to 0.004-inch minimum, and 0.005-inch maximum clearance between valve stems and tappet ("1" and "4," fig. 16). Use thickness gage to determine clearance; recheck (correcting if necessary) clearance after lock nut has been securely tightened.

(6)   Adjust exhaust valve tappets to 0.006-inch minimum, and 0.007-inch maximum clearance between valve stems and tappet. Use thickness gage to determine clearance; recheck (correcting if necessary) clearance after lock nut has been securely tightened.

(7)   Before turning down valve spring covers, inspect paper gasket between each cover and tappet guide. If broken or damaged, fit a new gasket to prevent oil leak. Turn down and securely tighten valve spring covers.

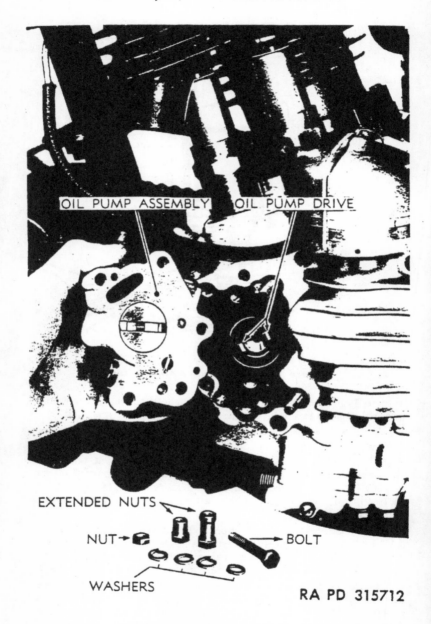

RA PD 315712

Figure 17—Oil Pump Removed

44. REPLACEMENT OF OIL FEED PUMP (fig. 17).

a. Removal.

(1) Disconnect oil tank feed pipe at oil tank. Install nipple cap on tank nipple to prevent oil from running out, or drain tank. Disconnect oil feed pipe from oil pump nipple.

(2) Oil pump is secured to engine gear case cover by one hexagon head bolt and three nuts. Two of the nuts are extra long to provide wrench clearance, and their location should be noted so they will be put back where they belong when reinstalling pump. After removing screw and nuts, remove pump. Unless a new pump gasket is available, take care not to damage or break the old one, as this is a very special gasket concerning both thickness and holes provided for oil channels. A "homemade" gasket may put oiling system completely out of commission.

b. Installing Oil Pump.

(1) Clean surface of pump body mounting on gear case cover and see that gasket is in good condition. Clean face of oil pump body.

(2) Start pump on mounting studs, turn engine slowly and press lightly against pump until driving dogs on end of cam gear shaft line up with and drop into driving slot in oil pump rotor.

(3) Insert hexagon-head bolt and lock washer, and install the three lock washers and nuts (two are long extension nuts) on pump mounting studs. Make sure to replace the two extra long nuts on the studs from which they were originally removed.

(4) Tighten mounting bolt and three nuts securely.

(5) Connect oil feed pipe to oil pump nipple. Remove nipple cap from tank nipple and connect upper end of oil feed pipe to this nipple. Tighten nipple nuts securely.

ENGINE—REMOVAL AND INSTALLATION

45. REMOVE ENGINE (figs. 18, 19, and 20).

a. A study of figures 18 and 19 will provide a good picture of the steps necessary for engine removal. Do not attempt any short cut methods, as this would consume more time and possibly cause damage to parts or unit assemblies.

(1) Disconnect battery ground wire at frame lug connection on right side of vehicle.

(2) To disconnect brake front rod from bell crank (located on right side of rear support rod), remove cotter pin and plain washer.

(3) Loosen footboard rear support stud nut and remove footboard front stud nut, then pull footboard outward to free right front end of safety guard. Disconnect brake front rod at bell crank. Remove bolt which secures front exhaust pipe clamp. Remove nut from rear support rod, freeing stop light switch and rear end of side bar. Remove nut ·from front support rod, freeing footboard and brake assembly for removal.

(4) Remove the two rear mounting bolts and drop rear end of skid plate (fig. 37).

(5) Remove muffler (par. 81).

(6) Disconnect oil pipe from tank and install nipple cap on oil tank feed pipe nipple to prevent oil from running out, or drain tank. Disconnect pipe from oil pump and remove oil pipe.

(7) Disconnect spark control wire at circuit breaker lever, and free control housing clamp at cylinder base.

(8) Disconnect brake rear rod from bell crank.

(9) Disconnect red wire and black wire from front end of relay; also green wire from generator terminal.

(10) Remove spark plugs.

(11) Remove engine top mounting (cylinder head bracket) bracket to frame lug bolt; this also frees front spark plug cable clamp. Pay particular attention to shim washers (if any) between cylinder head bracket and frame lug; these will have to be installed in the original position.

(12) Remove lever bottom bolt, freeing gear shifter lever from shifter rod.

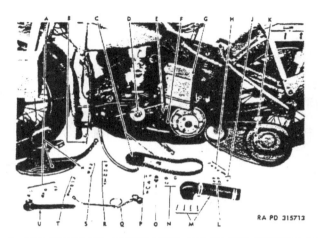

RA PD 315713

A—LEFT FOOTBOARD, CLUTCH PEDAL AND SIDEBAR ASSEMBLY AND MOUNTING NUTS AND WASHERS

B—SPARK CONTROL WIRE AND HOUSING

C—ENGINE SPROCKET, KEY, NUT AND FRONT DRIVE CHAIN

D—ENGINE SPROCKET SHAFT

E—REAR SUPPORT ROD

F—INNER CHAIN GUARD

G— AIR CLEANER AND BRACKET ASSEMBLY

H—OUTER CHAIN GUARD REAR MOUNTING BOLT, WASHER, SPRING, NUT AND COTTER PIN

J—SPARK COIL REAR TERMINAL NUT, WASHER AND SCREW

K—OUTER CHAIN GUARD

L—AIR CLEANER BRACKET UPPER MOUNTING BOLT NUTS AND WASHERS

M—AIR CLEANER HOSE AND CARBURETOR FITTING ASSEMBLY AND MOUNTING SCREWS

N—ENGINE LEFT REAR BASE MOUNTING BOLT CASTLE NUT, WASHERS AND COTTER PIN

O—REAR SUPPORT ROD EXTENDED NUT

P—INNER CHAIN GUARD MOUNTING SCREWS AND LOCKS

Q—FUEL PIPE AND STRAINER ASSEMBLY

R—ENGINE LEFT FRONT BASE MOUNTING BOLT, WASHERS, CASTLE NUT AND COTTER PIN

S—GEAR SHIFTER AND ROD ATTACHING BOLT, WASHER AND NUT

T—TANK, LOWER FRONT MOUNTING BOLT, WASHERS AND NUT

U—ENGINE SPROCKET NUT WRENCH

RA PD 315713B

Figure 18—Disassembly for Engine Removal—Left Side

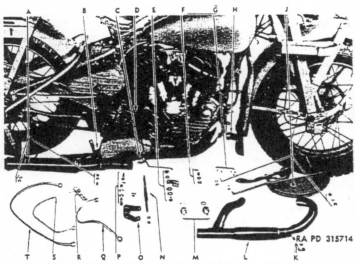

A—MUFFLER ASSEMBLY AND MOUNTING BOLTS AND NUTS

B—SKID PLATE

C—STOP LIGHT SWITCH

D—REAR BRAKE ROD FRONT END

E—CYLINDER BRACKET AND FRAME MOUNTING BOLT, SPACING
    WASHERS, SPARK CABLE CLIP AND NUT

F—ENGINE RIGHT FRONT BASE MOUNTING BOLT CASTLE NUT,
    WASHERS AND COTTER PIN

G—RELAY TERMINAL SCREWS AND WASHERS

H—SAFETY GUARD END

J—RIGHT FOOTBOARD, BRAKE PEDAL AND SIDEBAR ASSEMBLY AND
    MOUNTING NUTS AND WASHERS

K—FRONT EXHAUST PIPE CLAMP, BOLT, WASHER AND NUT

L—EXHAUST PIPE ASSEMBLY

M—SPARK PLUGS AND GASKETS

N—REAR SUPPORT ROD, WASHER AND NUT

O—BRAKE ROD BELLCRANK

P—ENGINE REAR BASE MOUNTING BOLTS, WASHERS, CASTLE NUT AND
    COTTER PIN

Q—OIL FEED PIPE

R—VENT PIPE HOLLOW BOLT AND WASHER

S—VENT PIPE

T—OIL RETURN PIPE   RA PD 3157148

Figure 19—Disassembly for Engine Removal—Right Side

(13)   Close fuel tank valve. Remove gasoline pipe from tank nipple and fuel filter nipple.

(14)   Disconnect throttle control wire at carburetor lever.

(15)   Disconnect air intake hose connection fitting from carburetor (four screws) and leave attached to hose. Remove air cleaner from mounting bracket (par. 78).

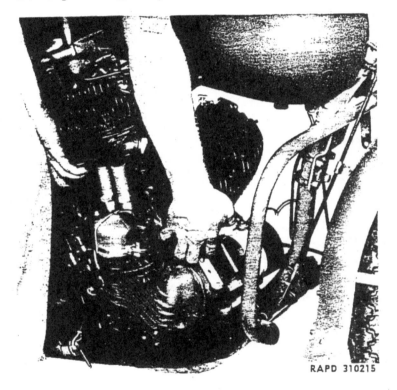

Figure 20—Removing Engine

(16)   Remove front chain guard (par. 102).

(17)   Remove engine sprocket (par. 65).

(18)   Remove two screws and locks securing inner chain guard to crankcase.

(19)   With $1\frac{3}{16}$-inch deep socket wrench slipped over rear footboard support rod stud, remove extended nut, and withdraw support rod from right side of vehicle.

(20)   To disconnect the circuit breaker to coil wire and shielding ground from coil rear terminals, disconnect oil pressure signal light wire from oil pressure switch terminal. It will be necessary to free air cleaner mounting bracket and swing it outward, to gain access to coil rear shielding ground terminal.

(21)   Engine mounting bolts are secured by cotter pins and castle nuts. Remove all engine mounting bolts, except the one under generator; this bolt cannot be removed without removing generator; merely push it up far enough to clear frame engine lug when engine is removed from frame.

(22)   Lift and remove engine from right side of frame.

46.   INSTALL ENGINE (figs. 18, 19, and 20).

a.   Installing the engine is generally the reverse of the procedure followed in engine removal. Pay close attention to the following procedure because checking and adjustment of controls and other items is necessary to satisfactory vehicle operation.

(1)   Lift engine into frame from right side of vehicle. Make sure that mounting bolt under generator is raised to clear frame engine lug.

(2)   Pass remaining three engine mounting bolts up from under side of frame lugs through crankcase lugs; install plain washers and castle nuts. Fit plain washer and castle nut on mounting bolt under generator. Securely tighten all four castle nuts and lock with cotter pins.

(3)   Connect circuit breaker to coil wire. Connect wire to coil rear terminal and ground shielding on coil case terminal.

(4)   Connect oil pressure switch wire to switch terminal.

(5)   Pass rear footboard support rod through frame lug from right side of vehicle and install the extended $13/_{16}$-inch nut.

(6)   Secure inner chain guard by attaching the two screws and locks mounting inner chain guard to engine base. Drift edge of locks into screw slots for security.

(7)   Install engine sprocket and front drive chain together. See that engine shaft is clean, sprocket taper clean, and that key is in place before tightening sprocket nut. Drift nut tight, using hammer on wrench.

(8)   Install outer front chain guard (par. 102).

(9)   Connect hose and fitting assembly by installing two bolts, washers, and nuts securing air cleaner to frame bracket; then install four screws securing hose fitting to carburetor. NOTE: *If cleaner frame bracket was loosened and shifted to gain access to coil rear terminals, securely mount bracket before installing air cleaner assembly.*

(10)   Connect throttle control wire to carburetor lever. Make sure that throttle closes fully when right grip is turned outward; and that throttle opens fully when grip is turned inward.

(11)   Install fuel pipe. Securely tighten union nuts on tank and fuel strainer nipples. Open fuel supply valve and check connections for leaks.

(12)   Connect gear shifter lever end to gear shifter rod by tightening bolt and nut.

(13)   Attach engine top mounting bracket (cylinder head bracket) to frame lug, exercising care in installing required number of thin shims, together with clamp for front spark plug cable, to fill space between bracket and frame lug before tightening bolt nut. NOTE: *Frame lug must be free from paint or grease to make clean "electrical" connection with plated shims and mounting bracket for adequate radio bonding.*

(14)   Before installing spark plugs, inspect for cleanliness and correct electrode adjustment. Service if necessary (par. 83). Replace gaskets to ensure tight joints.

(15)   Connect red and black wires to relay; connect green wire to generator terminal marked "SWITCH." Refer to wiring diagram (fig. 73).

(16)   Attach rear brake rod to bell crank. Install plain washer and secure with cotter pin.

(17)   Connect spark control wire to circuit breaker lever and secure control wire housing clamp under cylinder base nut. Make sure that spark advances fully (lever inward) when control grip (left handle bar) is turned inward, and that spark retards fully when control grip is turned outward. Make needed adjustment at control wire and lever connection.

(18)   Remove nipple cap from tank oil pipe nipple (if one was used) and connect oil feed pipe, securely tightening union nuts at tank and oil pump.

(19)   Position exhaust pipe and muffler assembly and attach rear hanger frame bolt, washer, and nut. Secure muffler front mounting bracket bolt, but do not tighten nut until skid plate rear bracket is located on this bolt.

(20)   Lift rear end of skid plate, secure rear mounting bracket and muffler front mounting bracket with bolt, washer, and nut. Attach skid plate left side bracket, tightening support rod nut and bracket bolt and nut.

(21)   Install right side footboard, sidebar, and brake pedal assembly. Install stop light switch bracket on rear support rod before placing lock washer and tightening nut. Attach front exhaust pipe clamp to sidebar. Install lock washer, and tighten sidebar front

support rod nut. Attach right end of front safety guard to sidebar with footboard front support stud. Replace lock washer, and tighten nut. Also tighten footboard rear support stud nut. Connect stop light switch control to brake foot pedal.

(22)   Attach brake front rod to bell crank: fit plain washer and secure with cotter pin.

(23)   Connect battery ground wire to frame lug on right side of vehicle.

b.   Check instrument panel signal lights for normal indications. and see that oil is in tank before starting engine.

CLUTCH

47. DESCRIPTION (fig. 21).

a. Clutch is of simple multiple-dry-disk type, having two steel disks and three lined disks, one of which provides spring action within disk pack to "cushion" clutch operation.

48. MAINTENANCE AND ADJUSTMENT (figs. 22, 23, 24, and 25).

a. If clutch adjustment is correctly maintained, clutch will cause very little trouble. Ease of gear shifting and service life of transmission gear shifter clutch dogs depend largely upon full disengagement of the clutch. Clutch adjustment is in two parts; namely, control linkage and spring tension. Do not adjust clutch spring tension before correcting control adjustment.

b. Clutch Control Linkage (fig. 22). Operation of foot pedal, control cable, and clutch release lever actuates the push rod through hollow transmission shaft, disengaging or engaging clutch at will. Correct adjustment to control cable and release lever must be made before push rod adjustment is made.

c. Clutch Control Adjustment (figs. 23, 24, 25, and 26).

(1) ADJUSTING CABLE LENGTH. With clutch in fully disengaged position (foot pedal heel down) the clutch release lever must clear the countershaft sprocket cover stud and/or nut by $\frac{1}{16}$ inch. Should clutch release lever strike sprocket cover and nut, clutch push rod movement is restricted, and clutch cannot be fully disengaged. Length of control cable must be adjusted to obtain $\frac{1}{16}$-inch clutch release lever and sprocket cover stud and/or nut clearance. To lengthen or shorten clutch control cable, cable adjustable end must be removed from foot pedal stud (figs. 23 and 24). With foot pedal in forward (toe down) position, remove cotter pin and washer retaining cable end. Release other end of cable from notch in clutch release lever by pressing release lever inward and lifting cable end out of notch. Rock the foot pedal to rear (heel down) position and work cable adjustable end off foot pedal stud. Loosen lock nut and turn cable end to right (clockwise) to shorten cable; turn to left (counter-

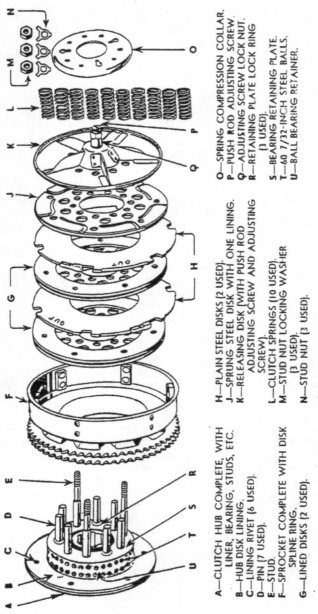

RAPD 310218

A—CLUTCH HUB COMPLETE, WITH
   LINER, BEARING, STUDS, ETC.
B—HUB DISK LINING.
C—LINING RIVET (6 USED).
D—PIN (7 USED).
E—STUD.
F—SPROCKET COMPLETE WITH DISK
   SPLINE RING.
G—LINED DISKS (2 USED).

H—PLAIN STEEL DISKS (2 USED).
J—SPRUNG STEEL DISK WITH ONE LINING.
K—RELEASING DISK (WITH PUSH ROD
   ADJUSTING SCREW AND ADJUSTING
   SCREW).
L—CLUTCH SPRINGS (10 USED).
M—STUD NUT LOCKING WASHER
   (3 USED).
N—STUD NUT (3 USED).

O—SPRING COMPRESSION COLLAR.
P—PUSH ROD ADJUSTING SCREW.
Q—ADJUSTING SCREW LOCK NUT.
R—RETAINING PLATE LOCK RING
   (3 USED).
S—BEARING RETAINING PLATE.
T—60 7/32-INCH STEEL BALLS.
U—BALL BEARING RETAINER.

Figure 21—Clutch, Disassembled

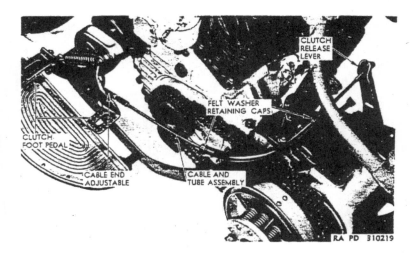

Figure 22—Clutch Control Linkage

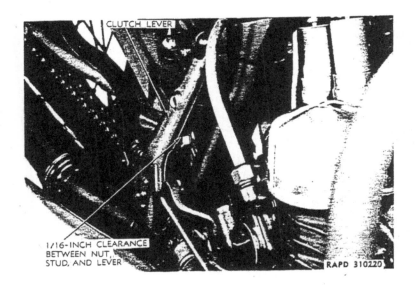

Figure 23—Clutch Lever and Stud Nut Clearance

Figure 24—Control Cable Length Adjustment

clockwise) to lengthen cable. Tighten lock nut, install cable end on
foot pedal stud; install washer and cotter pin, and install other end
of cable in clutch release lever notch.

(2) ADJUSTING CLEARANCE OF CLUTCH RELEASE LEVER AND
PUSH ROD (fig. 25). With clutch release lever and sprocket cover
stud clearance correctly adjusted (step (1) above), clutch release
lever must have between $\frac{1}{8}$-inch and $\frac{1}{4}$-inch free play at end where

Figure 25—Clutch Adjustments

control cable engages lever notch (fig. 25). This free play ensures a fully engaged clutch without pressure on clutch release bearing. Adjustment is made by means of push rod adjusting screw located in clutch outer disk. Remove two screws which secure inspection hole cover to chain guard (fig. 25). If clutch release lever has less than ⅛-inch free play at end of cable, loosen push rod adjusting screw lock nut and turn push rod adjusting screw to the left (counterclockwise) to increase amount of free play. If clutch release lever has more than ¼-inch free play at end of cable, turn adjusting screw to the right (clockwise) to decrease amount of free play. Tighten lock nut after correct adjustment is obtained. Replace inspection hole cover. CAUTION: *If end of clutch release lever has no free play as explained above, clutch will not hold when fully engaged. If too much free play is allowed, clutch will drag when disengaged; consequently, transmission gears will shift hard, clash, and eventually become damaged.*

SPRING TENSION ADJUSTING NUTS

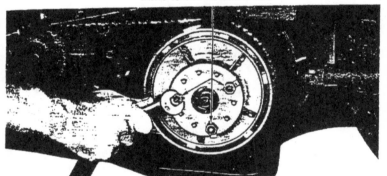

RA PD 310223

Figure 26—Adjusting Clutch Spring Tension

d. **Adjusting Clutch Spring Tension** (fig. 26). If clutch slips (does not hold when starting engine or with vehicle in operation) after controls have been correctly adjusted (step c (1) and (3) above), spring tension must be increased. NOTE: *Do not increase spring tension any more than actually required to make clutch hold.*

(1)   Remove front outer chain guard (par. 102).

(2)   Bend down lock lips to free the three clutch adjusting nuts.

(3)   Turning nuts to right (clockwise) increases clutch spring tension. Tighten (turn to right) all three adjusting nuts, one-half turn at a time, until clutch holds. Test clutch after each half-turn

of the three adjusting nuts by cranking engine. Usually a clutch that holds without any noticeable slippage when cranking engine, also holds on the road.

(4) After clutch spring tension adjustment is made, bend up nut lock lips to secure adjusting nuts. Replace any broken or badly damaged locks.

(5) When a new clutch is originally assembled and adjusted, the distance from the inner edge of shoulder on spring collar to face of outer (releasing) disk is $1\frac{3}{32}$ inches (fig. 27). In any case, do not tighten the three adjusting nuts to the point where inner edge of shoulder of spring collar is closer than $\frac{7}{8}$ inch to face of outer (releasing) disk. If compressed more, clutch probably cannot be fully disengaged.

Figure 27—Measuring Distance Between Spring Collar and Disk

(7) If clutch still does not hold, after correct control and spring tension adjustments have been made, clutch "pack" assembly must be replaced (par. 49).

(8) After making clutch spring tension adjustment, replace outer front chain guard (par. 102).

49. REMOVAL OF DISKS (figs. 28, 29, and 30).

a. Clutch disks can be removed for inspection, cleaning, and/or replacing. Springs can be removed for checking and/or replacing

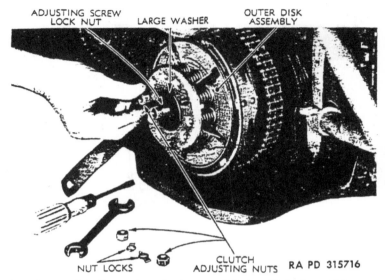

ADJUSTING SCREW LOCK NUT   LARGE WASHER   OUTER DISK ASSEMBLY

NUT LOCKS   CLUTCH ADJUSTING NUTS   RA PD 315716

Figure 28—Removing Spring and Outer Disk Assembly

without disturbing sprocket, which is integral with clutch shell. It is advisable to remove releasing (outer) disk, springs, and collar as an assembly because it is difficult to correctly aline, hold in place, and reassemble springs in this unit. If springs show signs of overheating, and appear to be "set," they should be removed, measured, and replaced if necessary (par. 50).

(1)   Remove outer front chain guard (par. 102).

(2)   Remove push rod adjusting screw lock nut. Place a large flat washer, approximately ⅛-inch thick, 1¾-inch in diameter with a ⅜-inch center hole, over push rod adjusting screw, and replace adjusting screw lock nut just removed (fig. 28). Tighten adjusting screw lock nut against large washer until the three clutch spring adjusting nuts are free. Bend nut lock down, remove the three adjusting nuts, and withdraw releasing (outer) disk and spring assembly as one unit. Remaining lined and plain steel disks can now be removed from sprocket and clutch shell unit without further disassembly (fig. 30). NOTE: *At time lined and plain disks are removed from shell, observe relative position of each disk in order of correct assembly.*

50.   INSPECTION OF DISKS AND SPRINGS.

a.   **Worn Disk Liners.** When disk liners are worn down flush (or nearly flush) with rivet heads, disk and liner assembly must be replaced.

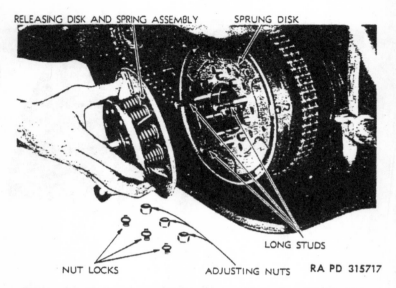

RELEASING DISK AND SPRING ASSEMBLY   SPRUNG DISK

LONG STUDS

NUT LOCKS   ADJUSTING NUTS   RA PD 315717

Figure 29—Outer Assembly Removed, Exposing Clutch Disks

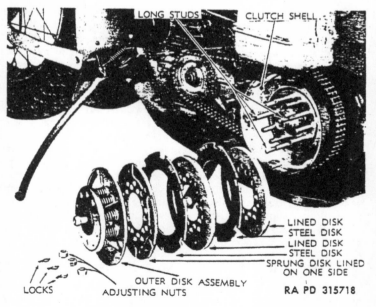

LONG STUDS   CLUTCH SHELL

LINED DISK
STEEL DISK
LINED DISK
STEEL DISK
SPRUNG DISK LINED
ON ONE SIDE

LOCKS   OUTER DISK ASSEMBLY
ADJUSTING NUTS   RA PD 315718

Figure 30—Clutch Disks, Removed

b. **Loose Liner Rivets.** If disk liner rivets are loose. replace disk and liner assembly with like assembly in new or good order.

c. **Oil-soaked Disk Liners.** If lined disks are not badly worn, but are oil-soaked, wash them thoroughly in clean gasoline and dry with air or heat.

d. **Shrunken or Weak Springs.** If clutch has been badly over-heated as a result of slippage, springs may be found in shrunken or weakened condition. Assuming disk liners are not badly worn, weakened springs are indicated when the three spring tension nuts have been tightened to make the clutch hold until the distance between spring collar and releasing (outer) disk is $\frac{7}{8}$ inch. If shrunken or weak springs are suspected, remove them for inspection.

(1) To remove springs, remove push rod adjusting screw lock nut. freeing spring collar and the 10 springs from the releasing (outer) disk assembly.

(2) Measure springs for free length. Free length of new clutch springs is approximately $1\frac{1}{2}$ inches (they may vary plus or minus $\frac{1}{32}$ inch). Old springs found to be shrunk $\frac{1}{8}$ inch (total free length of spring is $1\frac{3}{8}$ inch or less) must be replaced with new springs. NOTE: *Before replacing springs, select 10 springs that do not vary more than $\frac{1}{32}$ inch to make up the assembly.*

(3) ASSEMBLING RELEASING DISK, SPRINGS, AND SPRING COLLAR. Place the 10 springs upright on releasing disk to centrally locate each of the 10 stud holes. Place spring collar (flanged edge down) over ends of springs, locating the collar plate "dimples" in ends of 7 of the springs. Place the large washer over push rod adjusting screw; tighten adjusting screw nut, and compress springs lightly. Turn assembly over and observe alinement of springs and disk holes. If necessary. insert a $\frac{3}{8}$-inch rod through holes to aline springs. Tighten down adjusting screw nut; assembly is now ready for complete clutch assembly.

51. INSTALLATION OF DISKS (figs. 30, 29. and 28).

a. It is important when assembling a clutch to start with a lined disk. Install the two steel disks so that the antirattle devices are staggered on splines in the shell, and the "sprung" disk (lined on one side) is the last of the pack, its lined side facing the steel disk. Before installing disks, see that bearing retaining plate lock rings ("R," fig. 21) are in place on the short studs, and are tight against the retaining plate. This is to prevent noise in the clutch.

(1) Install one of the two lined disks on clutch hub studs first.

(2) Next. engage one of the two steel disks with the splines within the clutch shell, with side stamped "OUT" facing outward.

(3) Install the remaining lined disk on the clutch hub studs.

(4) Engage remaining steel disk with shell splines with "OUT" side facing outward.

(5) Install "sprung" (one side lined) steel disk, lined side inward, on clutch hub studs.

(6) It will be noted that the three long, threaded-end, clutch hub studs are not spaced an equal distance apart. It will also be noted that the three holes (keyhole shaped) in the spring collar are not spaced equidistantly. Therefore, when installing releasing disk and spring assembly on clutch hub studs, the three threaded studs and holes in spring collar must be alined. Install assembly on studs, replace the three nut locks, replace the three adjusting nuts, and tighten all three evenly until the distance between shoulder of spring collar and face of releasing disk is $1\frac{1}{32}$ inch (fig. 27).

(7) Remove the large washer and replace push rod adjusting screw lock nut. Do not attempt adjustment of clutch release lever and push rod adjusting screw until outer front chain guard and footboard have been installed.

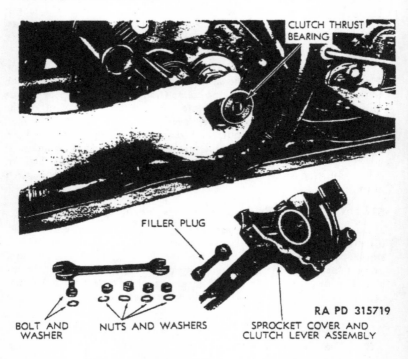

CLUTCH THRUST BEARING

FILLER PLUG

BOLT AND WASHER   NUTS AND WASHERS

RA PD 315719

SPROCKET COVER AND CLUTCH LEVER ASSEMBLY

Figure 31—Removing Clutch Releasing Bearing Assembly

(8)   Install outer front chain guard (par. 102).

(9)   Check controls and clutch adjustment. If necessary, correct according to paragraph 48.

52.   REPLACEMENT OF CLUTCH RELEASE BEARING (fig. 31).

a.   Clutch release lever acts against a thrust bearing and push rod assembly which actuates clutch releasing disk.

b.   **Remove Clutch Release Bearing.** Engage clutch fully (foot pedal toe down) and disengage clutch control cable end from slotted end of clutch release lever.

(1)   Loosen rear chain guard by removing cap screw which retains rear chain oil pipe and secures front end of rear drive chain guard to transmission countershaft sprocket cover.

(2)   Remove the four nuts which secure sprocket cover to transmission.

(3)   Remove filler plug.

(4)   Hold down starter crank with screwdriver.

(5)   Remove sprocket cover and clutch release lever assembly. It may be necessary to pry cover off studs. With cover removed, clutch release bearing is exposed.

(6)   Withdraw clutch release bearing and push rod assembly from transmission shaft.

c.   **Install Clutch Release Bearing.**

(1)   Insert push rod with clutch release bearing assembly into transmission shaft hole, as far as rod will go. See that bearing is clean and well greased.

(2)   Install sprocket cover. Securely tighten the four nuts.

(3)   Install cap screw which secures rear chain guard end and chain oiler pipe clamp to sprocket cover.

(4)   Engage clutch control cable end in slotted end of clutch release lever.

(5)   Check clutch release lever for free play at end of cable.

Section XIV

TRANSMISSION

53. DESCRIPTION.

a. Transmission has three speeds: low. second. and high. and is of the constant-mesh. non-selective type. High gear is direct drive. Since "dogs" on gear shifter clutches are used to engage transmission gears, it is of great importance that vehicle clutch is correctly adjusted. Clutch must be fully disengaged when shifting gears. to prevent clashing of gears, and possible damage to the shifter clutch "dogs" and transmission gears. It is also important that gear shifter control linkage be kept in correct adjustment to ensure full engagement of shifter clutch driving dogs in all positions. thus preventing possible damage caused by dogs jumping out of engagement under driving load. Close fitting and needle roller bearings. within the transmission. necessitate use of engine oil (seasonal grade) in transmission case for adequate lubrication.

54. CONTROL LINKAGE (fig. 32).

a. **Transmission Shifted to Adjust Front Drive Chain.** The transmission is located to receive power from front (engine) drive chain and transmit power through rear drive chain to rear wheel. and is movable on its mounting for adjustment of the front (engine) drive chain. When front (engine) drive chain is adjusted. transmission gear shifter control linkage is affected. Therefore. after each front drive chain adjustment. gear shifter control linkage must be checked. and. if necessary. correctly adjusted to ensure proper gear shifting with full engagement of the gear shifter clutch driving "dogs" as well as prevent transmission from jumping out of gear under load.

b. **Checking Gear Shifter Control Linkage.** Before making adjustment to gear shifter control linkage. make the following checks: See that all linkage points from transmission gear shifter lever to gear shifter hand lever are well oiled and free-working. Check hand lever pivot bolt nut for tightness. Observe whether there is binding or interference with shifter rod at any point in the shifting range; this sometimes results from a bent shifter rod. Check whether or not shifter rod is correctly adjusted so that when hand lever is moved to any gear position in tank shifter guide, transmission lever moves to the proper position to fully engage shifter clutch dogs and shifter cam spring plunger in cam-locating notch (inside transmission).

Figure 32—Adjusting Gear Shifter Rod

c. Adjusting Gear Shifter Control Linkage (fig. 32).

(1) Set hand lever in "N" (neutral) position in shifter guide.

(2) Remove nut and bolt to disconnect shifter rod from hand lever.

(3) With slight backward and forward movement of shifter rod, carefully "feel" transmission lever into exact position where shifter cam spring plunger (inside transmission) seats fully in cam-locating notch.

(4) Next, see that hand lever is in exact "N" (neutral) position in tank shifter guide.

(5) Readjust length of shifter rod by loosening rod end lock nut, and turning rod end (onto or off rod as necessary) until its bolt hole lines up with bolt hole in hand lever.

(6) Replace bolt and tighten nut.

(7) CHECK ADJUSTMENT. It is advisable to shift hand lever into "L" (low) and "S" (second) gear positions and check shifter rod adjustment to be sure of having best all-round adjustment.

(8) When shifter clutches become worn or damaged to the extent of jumping out of engagement under driving load, even though shifter control linkage is correctly adjusted, transmission must be removed and referred to higher authority for service.

55. REPLACEMENT OF FOOT STARTER CRANK.

a. Remove.

(1) Remove starter crank clamp bolt nut and remove bolt from crank.

(2) Pull starter crank off squared shaft.

b. Install. In installing foot starter crank, notch (for clamp-bolt clearance) must be in upward position in squared shaft to put return spring tension on crank.

(1) Use a 5/8-inch, open-end wrench and turn square shaft counterclockwise until bolt slot is upward. Hold shaft in this position and press starter crank onto shaft until clamping bolt can be inserted.

(2) Insert clamp bolt with bolt head toward rear wheel (crank in upward position) to provide clearance when starter crank is operated.

(3) Fit lock washer and nut and tighten nut securely.

56. REPLACEMENT OF STARTER CRANK SPRING (fig. 33).

a. Starter crank spring fits rather snugly behind rear edge of countershaft sprocket cover; however, it can be removed and installed without removing sprocket cover.

b. Remove.

(1) Remove foot starter crank (par. 55).

(2) With the blade of a screwdriver or with pliers, pry hooked end of spring off stud. NOTE: *If spring is broken, this operation will not be necessary.* Pull on spring end, at same time prying spring free of sprocket cover so as to pull spring off square shaft.

c. Install.

(1) Turn squared shaft so that clamp bolt notch is in bottom position. Engage square hole in spring on shaft with the hooked spring end to rear, in line with starter spring stud. Work spring onto

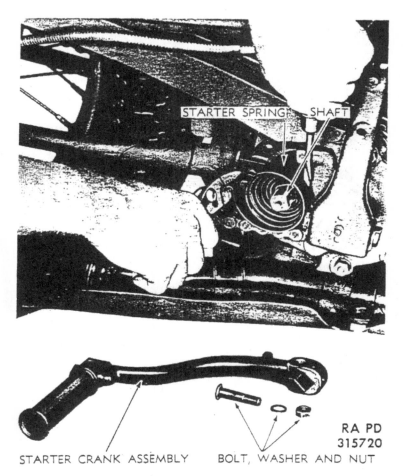

Figure 33—Removing Starter Crank Spring

shaft, prying it to rear to clear sprocket cover. Press all the way on squared shaft.

(2) Hook end of spring in place on spring stud.

(3) Install foot starter crank (par. 55).

57. REMOVE TRANSMISSION (figs. 34 and 35).

a. Transmission and clutch are assembled in one unit and must be removed and installed together. To make sure trouble is in trans-

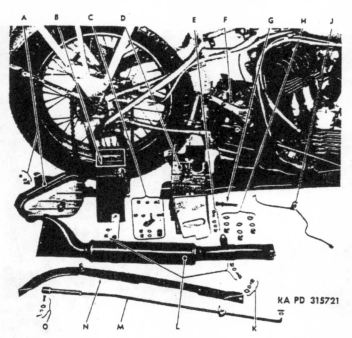

A—TOOL BOX AND BRACKET ASSEMBLY AND MOUNTING BOLT, WASHER AND NUT

B—BATTERY

C—BATTERY BOX REAR MOUNTING BOLTS, WASHERS, FITTINGS AND NUTS

D—BATTERY BOX ASSEMBLY AND COVER

E—BATTERY BOX FRONT MOUNTING BOLT, WASHERS AND NUT

F—TRANSMISSION AND CLUTCH ASSEMBLY

G—FRONT CHAIN ADJUSTING SCREW

H—TRANSMISSION MOUNTING STUD NUTS AND WASHERS

J—REAR CHAIN OILER PIPE

K—REAR CHAIN GUARD FRONT MOUNTING BOLT AND WASHERS

L—MUFFLER ASSEMBLY AND ATTACHING BOLT, WASHERS AND NUTS

M—REAR BRAKE ROD ASSEMBLY, WASHER AND COTTER PIN

N—REAR CHAIN GUARD

O—REAR BRAKE CLEVIS PIN, WASHERS AND COTTER PIN

RA PD 315721B

Figure 34—Disassembly for Transmission Removal from Right Side

mission, check clutch adjustment (par. 48) and transmission control linkage (par. 54) before replacing a faulty unit.

b. Remove.

(1)   Drop rear end of skid plate (par. 111).

(2)   Remove front chain guard (par. 102).

(3)   Remove oil bath air cleaner and mounting bracket (par. 80). Lower bracket bolt also secures clutch cable tube to frame tube bracket on left side.

(4)   Remove engine sprocket and front drive chain (par. 65).

(5)   Remove the two mounting screws and locks in engine case to free inner front chain guard.

(6)   Remove tool box from mounting bracket (par. 106). Remove bracket from frame.

(7)   Remove rear brake rod (par. 96).

(8)   Remove rear drive chain (par. 63).

(9)   Remove rear drive chain guard (par. 102). Remove rear chain oiler pipe after disconnecting at oil pump.

(10)   Remove battery box (par. 105).

(11)   Remove nut, washer, and bolt securing clutch tube assembly bracket to frame bracket on right side of vehicle. Disengage clutch operating cable end from end of clutch release lever and remove cable and tube assembly.

(12)   Remove gear shifter rod by disconnecting at hand shifter lever and at transmission gear shifter lever.

(13)   Remove the three transmission mounting stud nuts, then remove lock washers and large plain washers (located under frame bracket), and lift transmission sufficiently to permit removal of front chain adjusting screw.

(14)   Loosen upper U-bolts on ignition coil mounting, then remove the lower U-bolt nuts and shift coil on frame tube as far as possible toward the front.

(15)   Remove transmission and clutch assembly from vehicle by lifting complete unit sufficiently to free mounting studs from frame bracket; then rotate top of transmission backward about $\frac{1}{4}$ turn (fig. 34) and remove unit from left side of frame (fig. 35).

58. INSTALL TRANSMISSION (figs. 34 and 35).

a. Install from Left Side. Working from left side of frame, tilt top of transmission backward, and as unit passes into position, rotate top forward, until unit is squarely in position and mounting studs pass through slots in frame mounting bracket.

(1)   Shift ignition coil mounting back into correct position and tighten U-bolt nuts.

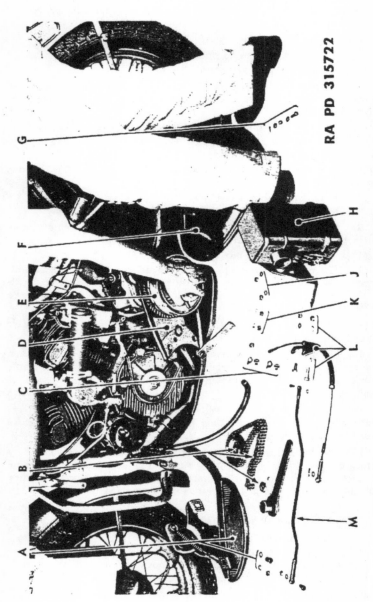

RA PD 315722

Figure 35—Disassembly for Transmission Removal from Left Side of Vehicle

(2)   Install front chain adjusting screw. Lift transmission to engage screw in frame notch.

(3)   Install large plain washers, lock washers, and nuts on the three transmission mounting studs. Do not tighten.

(4)   Install gear shifter rod by connecting to hand shifter lever and transmission gear shifter lever.

(5)   Install clutch operating cable and tube assembly. Connect cable end to clutch release lever. Position tube assembly bracket to frame bracket and install bolt, washer, and nut to hold in place.

(6)   Install battery box (par. 105).

(7)   Install rear drive chain guard (par. 102).

(8)   Install rear drive chain (par. 63).

(9)   Install rear brake rod (par. 96).

(10)   Install tool box bracket and tool box (par. 106).

(11)   Secure inner front chain guard to engine base by installing screw locks and screws. After screws are tightened, drift edge of each lock into screw slot for security.

(12)   Install engine sprocket and front drive chain (par. 65).

(13)   If necessary, adjust front drive chain (par. 59).

(14)   Securely tighten transmission mounting stud nuts.

A—LEFT FOOTBOARD, CLUTCH PEDAL AND SIDEBAR ASSEMBLY AND MOUNTING NUTS AND WASHERS

B—ENGINE SPROCKET, NUT, KEY AND FRONT CHAIN

C--INNER CHAIN GUARD MOUNTING SCREWS AND LOCKS

D—INNER CHAIN GUARD

E—TRANSMISSION AND CLUTCH ASSEMBLY

F—OUTER CHAIN GUARD

G—OUTER CHAIN GUARD REAR MOUNTING BOLT, WASHER, SPRING, NUT AND COTTER PIN

H—AIR CLEANER AND BRACKET ASSEMBLY

J—AIR CLEANER BRACKET UPPER MOUNTING BOLT NUTS AND WASHERS

K—SPARK COIL LOWER MOUNTING U-BOLT NUTS AND WASHERS

L--CLUTCH CABLE AND HOUSING ASSEMBLY AND MOUNTING BOLTS, WASHERS AND NUTS

M—GEAR SHIFTER ROD ASSEMBLY WITH ATTACHING BOLT, WASHERS, PIN AND NUT

RA PD 315722B

Legend for Figure 35—Disassembly for Transmission Removal from Left Side of Vehicle

(15) Install outer front chain guard cover (par. 102). Connect rear chain oiler pipe to oil pump.

(16) Install air cleaner and mounting bracket, air hose, and connections (par. 79).

(17) Lift skid plate into position and install two mounting bolts, lock washers, and nuts.

(18) Check gear shifter control, and, if necessary, adjust linkage (par. 54).

(19) Check rear drive chain adjustment and adjust if necessary (par. 60).

(20) Check rear brake adjustment. If necessary, adjust rear brake linkage (par. 96).

(21) Check clutch controls and adjust if necessary (par. 48).

(22) Before operating vehicle, see that transmission oil level is up to filler opening (vehicle standing upright).

CHAINS AND SPROCKETS

59. ADJUST FRONT CHAIN (figs. 36, 37, and 38,).

a. At the time front chain adjustment is made, inspect chain for correct lubrication and, if necessary, adjust front chain oiler (par. 61).

b. Chains wear unevenly and some stretch may result, making tight and loose sections. For this reason, engine must be turned and chain rotated to position of least slack at the time adjustment is made.

c. A correctly adjusted front chain has $\frac{1}{2}$-inch, or slightly more, free up-and-down movement midway between sprockets, at inspection hole. Chain must never be run taut (no slack at tightest point). Chain must never be allowed to run loose enough to cause jerky, noisy action and/or strike the chain guard.

d. Adjustment of front chain is made by shifting transmission on its mounting base. This will affect adjustment of gear shifter control linkage, clutch control linkage, and rear chain.

e. How to Adjust Front Chain.

(1) Remove inspection hole cover by removing screws and lifting cover from front outer chain guard, exposing chain (fig. 36).

(2) Obtain tightest chain position by rotating chain to position of least slack. Test amount of slack by lifting and depressing chain with finger. Use a free up-and-down motion of the finger to make this test.

(3) Loosen the three transmission mounting stud nuts underneath transmission mounting base. (It is not necessary to drop skid plate to reach stud nuts (fig. 37).) Transmission can now be shifted on its mounting base by means of adjusting screw, head of which protrudes through notch of frame fitting, located at rear of transmission (fig. 38).

Figure 36—Front Chain Inspection Hole Cover Removed

(4) Turn adjusting screw clockwise (to the right) to move transmission backward and tighten front chain. Turn adjusting screw counterclockwise (to the left) to move transmission forward and loosen front chain.

(5) After moving transmission by means of adjusting screw, check front chain adjustment; then securely tighten the three transmission mounting stud nuts and again check chain adjustment, as tightening stud nuts sometimes changes chain adjustment.

(6) After front chain adjustment has been made, securely tighten the three transmission mounting stud nuts.

(7) Install front chain inspection hole cover and tighten screws.

(8) Check shifter lever control linkage adjustment (par. 54).

(9) Check clutch control linkage adjustment (par. 48).

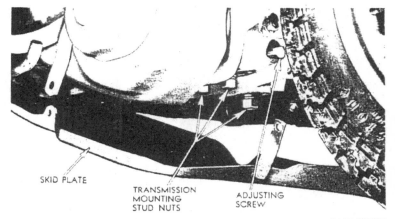

SKID PLATE

TRANSMISSION
MOUNTING
STUD NUTS

ADJUSTING
SCREW

RAPD 310234

**Figure 37—Skid Plate Dropped to Show Location of
Transmission Mounting Nuts**

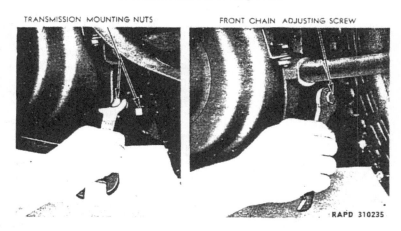

TRANSMISSION MOUNTING NUTS

FRONT CHAIN ADJUSTING SCREW

RAPD 310235

**Figure 38—Transmission Mounting Nuts and Chain
Adjusting Screw**

60. ADJUST REAR CHAIN AND ALINE REAR WHEEL (fig.
39).

a. In moving transmission backward on its mounting to tighten
front chain, the rear chain will be loosened. Rear chain must then
be adjusted by moving rear wheel backward. When rear wheel is

moved either forward or backward, adjustment of the rear wheel brake is affected.

b.   When checking rear chain for slack midway between the sprockets, turn wheel and rotate chain to position of least slack. Use free up-and-down movement of finger to lift chain and depress it to determine tightest position.

c.   At position of least slack, a correctly adjusted rear chain has ½-inch, or slightly more, free up-and-down movement midway

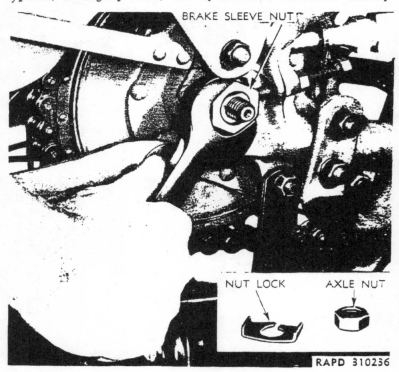

BRAKE SLEEVE NUT

NUT LOCK   AXLE NUT

RAPD 310236

Figure 39—Brake Sleeve Nut

between sprockets. Chain must never be run taut (no slack at tightest point). Chain must never be allowed to run loose enough to cause jerky operation and/or strike the chain guard or other chassis parts.

d.   At the time rear chain adjustment is made, inspect chain for correct lubrication and if necessary, adjust rear chain oiler (par. 61).

e.   Rear chain adjustment and rear wheel alinement are both made by means of the rear wheel adjusting screws. Therefore, adjustment of either the chain or the wheel alinement can affect adjustment of the other, making it necessary to consider both adjustments at the same time.

(1)   Remove rear axle nut and lock washer (right side of vehicle).

(2)   Loosen brake sleeve nut enough to allow brake assembly to slide backward or forward in frame mounting (fig. 39).

(3)   Loosen the two (right and left side) rear wheel adjusting screw lock nuts.

(4)   Turn wheel adjusting screws clockwise (to right) to move wheel and sprocket backward. This tightens chain. NOTE: *If chain is too tight, turn wheel adjusting screws counterclockwise (to left) so that wheel can be shifted forward. This will loosen chain.* Always turn the two wheel adjusting screws an equal number of turns in order to keep wheel alined.

(5)   Check correct alinement of wheel by noting that tire (not tire rim) runs approximately midway between lower rear frame tubes at the point where tubes join transmission mounting. It is desirable to have tire run slightly closer (not more than $\frac{1}{16}$ in.) to right than to left side lower tube. A further check of alinement is observing that rear sprocket runs centrally in chain. CAUTION: *If rear wheel is not correctly alined, vehicle steering will be affected, and sprockets will wear excessively on one side.*

(6)   With adjustment of chain and wheel alinement completed, securely tighten wheel adjusting screw lock nuts, and brake sleeve nut; replace axle lock washer and nut, tightening nut.

(7)   Recheck adjustment of chain as tightening brake sleeve nut and axle nut sometimes changes the chain adjustment.

(8)   After tightening rear chain, rear brake may be found too tight. Check and correct brake adjustment (par. 96).

61.   CHAIN OILERS (fig. 40).

a.   Both front and rear chains are automatically lubricated by engine oil pumps. Chain oilers are adjustable and may need occasional readjustment to meet lubrication requirements of varied operating conditions. Chains under most operating conditions require a very small amount of oil; therefore, chain oilers require very fine adjustment to supply just enough oil without waste.

b.   When adjusting chain oilers, it is advisable to add or remove only one thin washer at a time and inspect chain again after vehicle has run approximately 100 miles, to determine whether or not further adjustment is necessary.

c.   If inspection of front chain through inspection hole reveals that chain is not getting enough oil, adjust front chain oiler as follows:

(1)   Add thin (0.002-inch thick) washer under head of front chain oiler adjusting screw (fig. 40). Do not remove any washers already under head of screw.

(2)   To check results, refer to step b above.

d.   Evidence of too much oil on front chain requires cutting down on chain oiler.

Figure 40—Chain Oilers

(1)   To adjust oiler, remove thin (0.002-inch thick) washer from under head of front chain oiler adjusting screw (fig. 40).

(2)   To check results, refer to step b above.

e.   If inspection reveals that rear chain is not getting enough oil, and that oil pipe end is open, is not bent, and is directed on chain; then the rear chain oiler must be adjusted.

(1)   Adjust oiler by adding thin (0.002-inch thick) washer under head of rear chain oiler adjusting screw (fig. 40). Do not remove any washers already under head of screw.

(2)   To check results, refer to step **b** above.

f.   Evidence of too much oil on rear chain (supplied by oiler) requires cutting down on chain oiler.

(1)   To adjust oiler, remove thin (0.002-inch thick) washer from under head of rear chain oiler adjusting screw (fig. 40).

(2)   To check results, refer to step **b** above.

g.   At 1000-mile intervals, loosen both front and rear chain oiler adjusting screws (fig. 40) two turns each. Do not remove screws. Start and idle engine 1 minute, then tighten screws firmly, but do not force. This operation serves to flush oiler control valves and rear chain oiler pipe.

62.   REPLACEMENT OF FRONT CHAIN.

a.   A new or original duplex front chain is endless, not provided with connecting link, and engine sprocket must be removed in order to remove or replace chain.

b.   Remove.

(1)   Remove outer front chain guard (par. 102).

(2)   Remove engine sprocket (par. 65). Chain can now be lifted off clutch sprocket.

c.   Install. When installing a new front chain and/or sprocket, it may be necessary to shift transmission ahead in order to get chain on (par. 59 **e**).

(1)   Clean engine shaft taper and sprocket hole.

(2)   Place chain on clutch sprocket teeth and install sprocket (par. 65).

(3)   Check chain adjustment (par. 59).

(4)   Install outer front chain guard (par. 102).

63.   REPLACEMENT OF REAR CHAIN (fig. 41).

a.   Remove. Support vehicle on rear stand. With transmission in "N" (neutral) position, turn rear wheel until chain connecting link is located on rear sprocket teeth, about straight back from axle.

(1)   Using pliers, lift split end of connecting link spring clip out of link pin notch, taking care not to damage spring clip. Remove spring clip from other link pin notch.

(2)   Pull off link side plate and push link out of chain ends. Replace connecting link and spring clip in one end of chain to prevent its loss.

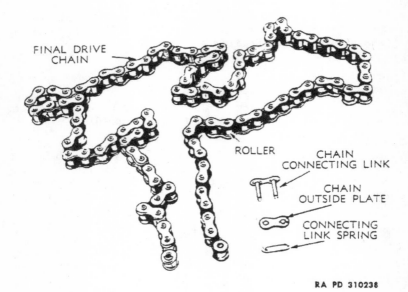

FINAL DRIVE
CHAIN

ROLLER   CHAIN
CONNECTING LINK

CHAIN
OUTSIDE PLATE

CONNECTING
LINK SPRING

RA PD 310238

Figure 41—Rear Drive Chain and Connecting Link

(3) Pull on lower half of chain, guiding upper part while it rotates around countershaft sprocket, until removed. If a new rear chain is to be installed, one end can be linked to the upper half end of old chain and can be pulled onto countershaft sprocket as old chain is removed.

b. **Install.** When installing a new rear chain and/or countershaft sprocket, it may be necessary to set rear wheel ahead in order to get chain on (par. 60).

(1) Start end of chain over countershaft sprocket teeth, using starter crank to turn sprocket. After chain end has reached front half of sprocket, it will be necessary to guide end under sprocket and out of sprocket cover. Center chain so that ends engage rear sprocket teeth, back of the axle.

(2) Install connecting link, side plate and spring clip. See that open end of spring clip is to the rear with regard to chain travel (like the end of an arrow). If original spring clip is bent or damaged, use a new one.

(3) Adjust rear chain (par. 60).

(4) Check rear brake adjustment (par. 96).

64. CHAIN REPAIR TOOL (fig. 42).

a. Damaged or broken chain links can be replaced with connecting (repair) links after bad links have been removed. To remove damaged or broken link, push out chain side plate pins with the chain repair tool (41-T-3320). Front chain is a double row of duplex chain; rear chain is a single row chain. The chain tool furnished in the tool kit is designed to accommodate both. To put a connecting link in the front chain, it will be necessary to remove front chain guard (par. 102).

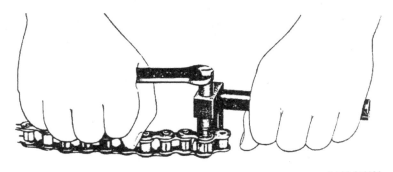

RAPD 310239

Figure 42—Chain Repair Tool in Use

b. When connecting (repair) links have been fitted to chain, make sure that spring clips are correctly and securely locked on link pin ends.

65. REPLACEMENT OF ENGINE SPROCKET.

a. **Remove.**

(1) Remove front outer chain guard (par. 102).

(2) Remove engine sprocket nut (right-hand thread). It will be necessary to strike wrench with a hammer to loosen nut.

(3) Give flat surface of engine sprocket, near outer edge, a light but sharp rap with a hammer, being careful not to strike and damage sprocket teeth. Take care not to lose sprocket shaft key.

b. **Install.** If new sprocket is being installed, it may be necessary to shift transmission forward to get chain to fit on sprockets (par. 59).

(1) Thoroughly clean engine shaft taper and see that key is in place. Clean sprocket taper hole, fit front chain on sprocket teeth, and rotate chain until keyway in sprocket lines up with key in engine shaft. Slip sprocket onto engine shaft, install nut, and tighten

securely. Strike wrench with a hammer to make sure sprocket nut is very tight.

(2)   Install front outer chain guard (par. 102).

66.   REPLACEMENT OF COUNTERSHAFT SPROCKET.

a.   Remove.

(1)   Remove foot starter crank (par. 55).

(2)   Remove starter crank spring (par. 56).

(3)   Remove countershaft sprocket cover (par. 52).

(4)   Bend back extension of sprocket nut lock.

(5)   Remove sprocket retaining nut. It will be necessary to strike wrench with a hammer to loosen nut.

(6)   Give sprocket a light but sharp rap with a hammer near outer edge, being careful not to strike the sprocket teeth, and remove sprocket from shaft taper. Do not lose the two sprocket shaft keys.

b.   Install.

(1)   Clean shaft taper and taper hole in countershaft sprocket. Install the two keys.

(2)   Install sprocket on shaft. Place rear chain on sprocket before installing sprocket cover.

(3)   Examine nut lock and, if badly damaged. use a new one.

(4)   Install sprocket retaining nut. Tighten by striking wrench with a hammer. NOTE: *This nut must be tight.* Bend up extension of nut lock against side of nut.

(5)   It will be easier to install starter crank spring at this step to avoid interference with sprocket cover.

(6)   Install sprocket cover.

(7)   Install starter crank.

Section XVI

FUEL SYSTEM

67. GENERAL.

a. Carburetor is of the side-outlet, plain-tube type with a fixed venturi. Fuel feed is by gravity from tank above. Carburetor has two manual controls: the throttle, which is operated by the right handle bar grip, and the choke, which is operated by a lever on the carburetor itself. The high speed fuel supply is governed by a fixed (non-adjustable) jet. The idling to medium speed (30 mph) fuel supply is governed by an adjustable (low speed) needle valve located on rear side of carburetor body.

68. CARBURETOR ADJUSTMENT (fig. 43).

a. Before attempting to adjust carburetor to correct faulty engine performance, attention should be given other items which have a direct bearing on and can affect carburetor adjustment as well as engine performance.

(1) Inspect fuel tank cap and make sure air vent is not plugged.

(2) See that throttle control adjustment is correct (par. 69).

(3) See that spark control adjustment is correct (par. 88).

(4) Drain and flush carburetor bowl (par. 73).

(5) Drain and flush fuel strainer (par. 72).

(6) Inspect air cleaner to see that passage of air through cleaner is not restricted by oil level being too high in oil cup, or by an excessive accumulation of dirt in filter elements (par. 76).

(7) Check manifold packing nuts and carburetor mounting screws for tightness.

(8) See that spark plugs are clean and that gaps are adjusted between 0.025 inch to 0.030 inch. If condition of spark plugs is questionable, install new ones.

(9) Check adjustment of valve tappets (par. 43).

(10) Check compression of both cylinders (par. 29 c

(11)   Check condition and adjustment of circuit breaker points (par. 84).

(12)   Check ignition to battery wiring connections (diagram fig. 48).

(13)   See that battery is not entirely discharged by turning on lights (tactical situation permitting) and observing brilliancy.

b.   A carburetor, once correctly adjusted, should require little, if any, readjusting. At most, it should not be necessary to adjust the low speed needle more than one or two notches either way to correct mixture to meet changes in weather conditions.

c.   Low Speed Adjusting Needle (figs. 43 and 44). Adjustment of this needle valve controls only idling and low speed (up to approximately 30 mph) fuel mixture. Turn needle valve down (to right) to make mixture leaner. Back out (to left) needle valve to make mixture richer. Needle valve is held in any desired position by a spring-and-ball plunger which engages notches in the needle adjusting screw.

d.   Complete Readjustment of Carburetor. A carburetor that is badly out of adjustment, and/or a new carburetor just installed, must be adjusted as follows:

(1)   Turn the low speed needle valve all the way down (to right).

(2)   Back needle valve out (to left) about three full turns. With needle valve in this position, engine will start, but mixture will probably be too rich.

(3)   Start engine as follows: After choke lever has been moved to normal open running position and engine is normally hot, correct adjustment of needle valve by turning needle valve down (to right) one notch at a time until mixture becomes so lean that engine misses, and is inclined to stop; then back out (to left) needle valve 5 to 10 notches, or until engine fires regularly with spark advanced and throttle closed (or as nearly closed as it can be set and still have engine running at idling speed).

(4)   Adjust throttle lever stop screw (fig. 43) as necessary to make engine idle at proper speed with throttle in fully closed position. Turning stop screw to the right makes engine idle faster. Turning stop screw to the left makes engine idle slower. Do not idle engine at the slowest possible speed, because an extremely slow idling adjustment causes hard engine starting. Changing idling speed with throttle stop screw is likely to change the low speed fuel mixture to some extent; therefore, it will be necessary to again check and correct the low speed needle valve adjustment (step (3) above).

(5)   Engine starting and all-round carburetion will be improved with low speed fuel adjustment slightly rich, rather than extremely lean.

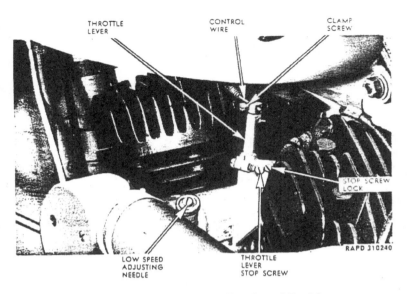

Figure 43—Throttle in Fully Closed Position

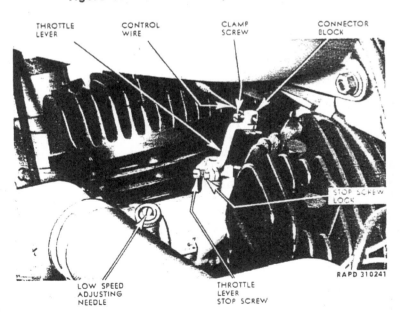

69. THROTTLE CONTROL WIRE ADJUSTMENT (figs. 43 and 44).

a. Carburetor throttle is opened and closed by means of the right handle bar grip, operating a control wire (within a housing) which connects to the throttle lever. Adjustment for full opening and closing of the throttle to correspond with full inward and outward motion of the handle bar grip is made at the junction of the control wire end and the throttle lever connection.

b. **Adjust Fully Closed Throttle** (fig. 43). See that there is about 1 inch distance between end of control wire housing and throttle lever when in fully closed position, so that housing end does not interfere with forward movement of throttle lever. If adjustment of control wire housing is necessary, refer to paragraph 101. Proceed with closed throttle adjustment.

(1) Loosen control wire clamp screw in connector block.

(2) Turn right handle bar grip outward as far as it will go; then turn it inward slightly. Holding throttle grip in this position, move throttle lever forward against its stop (closed position) and secure control wire in connector block with clamp screw. Check closing of throttle after tightening control wire set screw. If necessary, reset the control wire in the connector block until throttle is closed with full outward grip movement.

c. **Adjust Fully Open Throttle** (fig. 44). Follow instructions under step b above, then:

(1) Turn right handle bar grip inward as far as it will go and see that throttle lever is against its stop in fully open position. If throttle does not open fully when grip is turned inward, reset the control wire in the connector block to correct the adjustment.

70. CARBURETOR REMOVAL.

a. **Remove Carburetor for Replacement Only.**

(1) Shut off fuel supply valve.

(2) Loosen connector block clamp screw and disconnect throttle control wire at throttle lever.

(3) Disconnect fuel feed pipe at strainer nipple.

(4) Loosen air cleaner hose clamp at carburetor air intake fitting, and remove four screws and air intake fitting from carburetor.

(5) Remove the three mounting bolts (from right side of vehicle) which secure carburetor to manifold flange. CAUTION: *Take care not to damage or lose gaskets found between carburetor flange and manifold flange, and/or ½-inch thick steel spacer fitted between carburetor and manifold on some models.*

(6) Remove carburetor.

(7) Remove fuel strainer assembly from carburetor bowl nipple.

71. CARBURETOR INSTALLATION.

a. When installing carburetor be sure to fit the ½-inch thick steel spacer (if one was originally fitted) between carburetor and manifold flanges. with two gaskets on one side and one gasket on the other side. Later models have a longer manifold neck. extending carburetor farther to the left, away from cylinders, and do not need the spacer.

(1) Install fuel strainer assembly on bowl nipple. Leave coupling nut loose until after fuel pipe is connected.

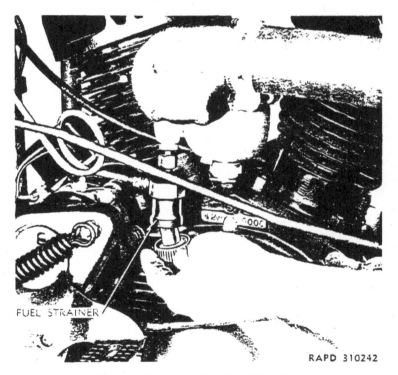

FUEL STRAINER

RAPD 310242

Figure 45—Removing Fuel Strainer

(2) To install carburetor on manifold. locate carburetor flange and two gaskets (½-inch steel spacer and gaskets if originally fitted) to aline with holes in manifold flange. and insert and securely tighten the three carburetor mounting screws. Use a ⁷₁₆-inch socket wrench, or a large screwdriver. to securely tighten these screws. NOTE: *If carburetor manifold is loose in manifold packing nuts (carburetor can be lifted and manifold turns in packing nuts), tighten manifold nuts securely, using manifold wrench (41-W-1570-10).*

(3)   Insert carburetor air intake fitting into end of air hose and mount fitting on carburetor with the four screws. Tighten air hose clamp.

(4)   Connect fuel pipe to fuel strainer nipple by tightening the union nut and also the strainer union nut on bowl nipple.

(5)   Attach throttle control wire to throttle lever connector block and adjust (par. 69).

(6)   Open fuel supply valve and observe for leaks.

(7)   Adjust carburetor (par. 68).

72. FUEL STRAINER (fig. 45).

a.   Cleaning.

(1)   Shut off fuel supply valve.

(2)   Unscrew cap from bottom of strainer body.

(3)   Lift strainer screen element with cork washer out of cap and clean thoroughly. Remove any dirt or sediment collected in cap. NOTE: *If compressed air is not available for cleaning, gasoline from the fuel pipe can be used for cleaning screen and cap.*

(4)   Install one cork washer in bottom of cap, set strainer screen element in place, and locate the other cork washer over screen element. Turn cap with screen element and washers onto bottom of strainer body, handtight.

b.   Remove Strainer Assembly.

(1)   Shut off fuel supply valve.

(2)   Disconnect fuel feed pipe at strainer body nipple.

(3)   Remove filter assembly from carburetor bowl nipple. It will be noted that coupling nut is an integral part of the filter body assembly.

c.   Install Strainer Assembly.

(1)   Install fuel strainer assembly on carburetor bowl nipple. Leave coupling nut loose until after fuel pipe is connected.

(2)   Connect fuel pipe to strainer body nipple and tighten union nut. Strainer coupling nut can now be tightened on bowl nipple.

(3)   Open fuel supply valve. Inspect fuel pipe and coupling nuts for leaks.

73. CARBURETOR BOWL CLEANING.

a.   Water from fuel, water moisture, and dirt entering air cleaner will settle in bottom of carburetor bowl and will interfere with engine starting and carburetion. At periodic intervals bowl must be drained. NOTE: *Before draining and flushing bowl, clean fuel strainer* (par. 72).

(1)   Support vehicle on jiffy (side) stand.

(2)   Shut off fuel supply valve.

(3)   Remove bowl drain screw. Let fuel, water, and dirt run out of bowl. With drain screw still removed, open fuel supply valve (turn to left) and leave open only a few seconds, to allow fresh gasoline to flush out bowl.

(4)   Replace bowl drain screw, taking care to avoid thread crossing. Set screw snug, but not tight enough to strip the threads.

74. FUEL PIPE.

a. Remove.

(1)   Shut off fuel supply valve.

(2)   Remove pipe union nut from tank nipple. Remove pipe after disconnecting union nut from fuel strainer body nipple.

b. Install. Fuel pipe must be installed without putting undue twist or strain on pipe or end fittings. Therefore, bend and/or shape pipe to "fit" between nipple connections before replacing and drawing up on union nuts.

(1)   Connect lower end of pipe to fuel filter body nipple. Do not tighten nut.

(2)   Connect upper end of pipe to tank nipple. Securely tighten this nut. Next, tighten union nut on strainer body nipple.

Section XVII

INTAKE AND EXHAUST SYSTEM

75. DESCRIPTION.

a. **Intake System.** The air intake system consists of oil bath air cleaner, connecting air hose, and carburetor intake hose fitting. This system is located on left side of vehicle.

b. **Exhaust System.** The exhaust system consists of muffler and tailpiece assembly, front exhaust pipe assembly, and rear exhaust pipe. Exhaust pipe ends are a slip fit in cylinder exhaust ports.

76. AIR CLEANER (figs. 46 and 47).

a. **General.** Air cleaner should not be submerged in water, nor should high-pressure stream be directed into cleaner louvers (where air enters on rear of body) when cleaning vehicle. Either water or dirt entering air cleaner in excessive quantities will raise the oil level in oil cup and choke off proper air supply to carburetor.

b. **Service.** With vehicle in normal use on hard-surfaced roads, clean and refill air cleaner oil cup with engine oil (seasonal grade) at least each time engine oil tank is drained and refilled. CAUTION: *Service more frequently under dusty conditions; daily under extremely dusty conditions. Check oil supply daily.*

(1) Hold oil cup with one hand and release (unlatch) oil cup retaining spring clips to remove oil cup.

(2) If oil in cup is clean, with no signs of dirt and grit in oil or cup, but the oil level is below the indicated level mark, add engine oil (seasonal grade) to bring level up to mark. NOTE: *If oil and cup are dirty, empty out oil and wash out cup with dry-cleaning solvent. Refill with clean engine oil (seasonal grade) to indicated level mark.*

(3) Before installing oil cup make sure that the oil cup gasket is in place and in good condition.

(4) Check baffle plate thumb screw for tightness.

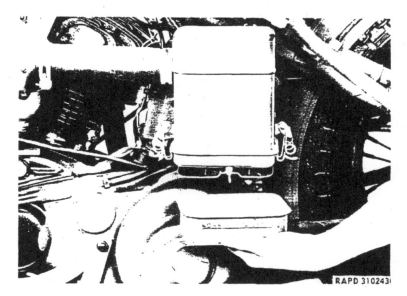

RAPD 310243

Figure 46—Air Cleaner Oil Cup Removed

(5)   Install oil cup, making sure that retaining spring clips are fully engaged in lip of oil cup and hold oil cup securely to cleaner body.

(6)   Oil bath air cleaners on earlier models are of "round" type, oil cup being secured to body with a metal clamp band and thumb screw. When oil cup is removed on this type of cleaner, the baffle plate will come out with the cup. Make sure that baffle plate is correctly installed and that gasket is in place when installing cup.

c.   **Maintenance** (fig. 47). The rectangular-type oil bath air cleaner is provided with two filter elements, retained in filter body by means of the baffle plate. If daily check reveals excessive accumulation of dirt and grit in oil and cup, filter elements must be removed and cleaned. NOTE: *Check several times daily under extremely dusty or sandy conditions.*

(1)   Hold oil cup with one hand and release (unlatch) oil cup retaining spring clips; remove cup.

(2)   Unscrew baffle plate thumb screw and remove baffle plate.

(3)   Filter elements may "bind" in cleaner body. If so, rap side of body with hand to loosen them; or, if necessary, withdraw elements from body with pliers or a hooked wire.

(4)   Check for presence and condition of gasket above the two filter elements (in filter body); also for oil cup gasket.

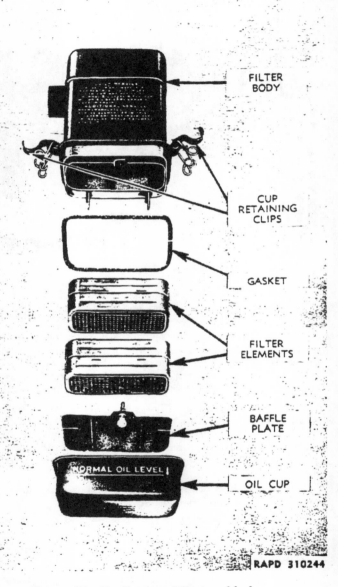

Figure 47—Air Cleaner, Disassembled

(5)   Clean both filter elements thoroughly in dry-cleaning solvent. Allow elements to dry out (use air hose if available).

(6)   Clean oil cup and refill to indicated level mark. Use clean engine oil (seasonal grade).

(7)   Dip one screen surface of each filter element about ½ inch into oil in the oil cup (to "oil wet" filter pack). Install the two filter elements, baffle plate, and oil cup immediately after "oil wetting" the filter elements. Make sure gaskets are in place. NOTE: *Do not add more oil to oil cup after elements have been dipped into it, because excess oil absorbed by elements will drip back into oil cup, bringing level back to normal.*

(8)   Round-type oil bath air cleaner used on earlier models does not have removable filter element. Complete cleaner body must be removed from vehicle, immersed and agitated in cleaning solvent to wash out dirt. After cleaning, allow filter element to dry (use air hose if available), then apply a few squirts of engine oil to inside of cleaner element, using oilcan. Refill cup, replace baffle plate and cup, securely tightening clamp band thumb screw.

77.   HOSE AND CARBURETOR FITTING.

a.   Remove. Carburetor intake and hose connection must be removed from carburetor to remove and/or install air hose.

(1)   Loosen screws in the two hose clamps.

(2)   Remove four screws retaining carburetor air intake fitting. Remove carburetor fitting from end of hose, and pull hose off air cleaner body connection.

b.   Install. Before installing air hose, inspect for breaks or faulty condition that might prevent airtight seal between air cleaner and carburetor fitting.

(1)   Install one end of hose on carburetor fitting. Do not tighten clamp screw,

(2)   Install other end of hose on air cleaner connection. Do not tighten clamp screw.

(3)   Install carburetor fitting. Securely tighten the four screws. Next, center air hose between carburetor fitting and air cleaner connection and securely tighten hose clamp screws.

78.   REMOVE AIR CLEANER.

a.   Loosen hose clamp screw at air cleaner body connection and remove two nuts and gear-toothed washers from bolts securing air cleaner assembly to frame bracket. NOTE: *Gear-toothed lock washers are also used under heads of the two mounting bolts. Withdraw cleaner from end of air hose.*

b.   The same procedure applies to round-type air cleaners used on earlier models.

79. INSTALL AIR CLEANER.

a. Engage air cleaner hose connection in end of hose and mount cleaner assembly on frame bracket with two bolts. gear-toothed lock washers. and nuts. Securely tighten mounting nuts. NOTE: *The plated (whitened) mounting bolts, four gear-toothed lock washers, and bolt nuts must effect a ground connection between bracket and filter mounting to insure adequate radio bonding.* Tighten air hose clamp screw at cleaner body connection.

b. The same procedure applies to round-type air cleaners used on earlier models.

80. REPLACEMENT OF AIR CLEANER MOUNTING BRACKET.

a. Air cleaner mounting bracket and air cleaner can be removed or installed as an assembly.

b. **Remove.**

(1) Loosen hose clamp connection at air cleaner body.

(2) Disconnect battery ground wire. This prevents shorting battery when removing cleaner bracket clamp bolt.

(3) Remove the two upper cleaner bracket frame clamp bolts.

(4) Remove lower mounting bolt. Cleaner lower bracket mounting and clutch cable tube mounting are secured to frame bracket by the same whitened radio bonding bolt, gear-toothed lock washers, and nut. Remove nut and drop bolt to free cleaner bracket.

c. **Install.**

(1) Engage air hose and cleaner body connection.

(2) Attach lower bracket first. Locate cleaner bracket so that hole lines up with bolt holes in frame bracket and clutch cable tube mounting. Pass whitened radio bonding bolt upward through bracket hole, install shakeproof lock washer, and securely tighten nut.

(3) Attach bracket to the two upper frame clips. Tighten the clamp bolt nuts.

(4) Connect battery ground wire.

(5) Tighten air hose clamp screw at cleaner connection.

81. EXHAUST SYSTEM.

a. **Remove Muffler Assembly.**

(1) Support vehicle on rear stand.

(2) Remove bolt from end of hanger bracket on left side of vehicle, and remove bolt from muffler clamp and skid plate bracket on right side of vehicle. Drop skid plate.

(3) Loosen nut and bolt on clamp which secures front end of muffler at exhaust pipe connection (clamp is attached to muffler).

(4) Remove muffler rear hanger bracket bolt nut. Pull muffler assembly free from exhaust pipe connection.

b. Install Muffler Assembly.

(1) Engage muffler pipe and exhaust pipe at muffler pipe clamp connection. Do not tighten clamp bolt nut as yet.

(2) Attach muffler rear hanger bracket to frame bracket bolt, installing lock washer, and tightening nut. NOTE: *It may be advisable to loosen hanger bracket on muffler so that muffler can be lined up for front end connection.*

(3) Tighten muffler and exhaust pipe clamp bolt nut and rear hanger nut.

(4) Raise skid plate into position and install right side mounting bolt which secures muffler front bracket and skid plate bracket to frame clip. Tighten all mounting nuts.

c. Remove Exhaust Pipes.

(1) Refer to step **a** (1), (2), (3) above.

(2) Remove right side footboard and brake pedal assembly as follows: Loosen footboard rear support stud nut, remove front support stud nut, and pull footboard outward to free end of safety guard. Remove bolt which secures front exhaust pipe clamp, and remove nut from rear support rod, freeing stop light switch and rear end of footboard sidebar. Remove nut from front support rod, and drop footboard and brake foot pedal assembly to provide clearance for exhaust pipe removal. Disengage rear exhaust pipe at cylinder port, at same time prying and pulling front exhaust pipe forward and downward to free from cylinder port. Both exhaust pipes can now be worked downward and removed from vehicle as an assembly.

d. Install Exhaust Pipes.

(1) Position exhaust pipe (front and rear) assembly, working it into position so that front pipe end slips into cylinder port; then, pry and force rear pipe end into rear cylinder port.

(2) Mount footboard, brake foot pedal, and sidebar assembly on support rods, installing washer and nut on front support rod.

(3) Position and mount stop light switch on rear support rod. See that spring and operating control wire exert a straight pull on switch plunger when foot pedal is operated.

(4) Install bolt, washer, and nut which secure front exhaust pipe clamp to footboard sidebar.

(5) To attach safety guard to sidebar, pull front end of footboard away from sidebar, line up holes in sidebar and safety guard end, then pass footboard support stud through both pieces, and secure with washer and nut.

(6) Tighten footboard rear support stud nut.

(7) To complete installation, follow procedure outlined in step **b** (1) through (4) above.

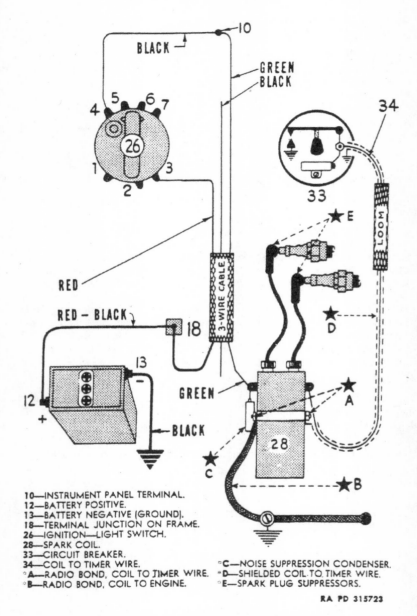

10—INSTRUMENT PANEL TERMINAL.
12—BATTERY POSITIVE.
13—BATTERY NEGATIVE (GROUND).
18—TERMINAL JUNCTION ON FRAME.
26—IGNITION—LIGHT SWITCH.
28—SPARK COIL.
33—CIRCUIT BREAKER.
34—COIL TO TIMER WIRE.
⚬A—RADIO BOND, COIL TO TIMER WIRE.
⚬B—RADIO BOND, COIL TO ENGINE.

⚬C—NOISE SUPPRESSION CONDENSER.
⚬D—SHIELDED COIL TO TIMER WIRE.
⚬E—SPARK PLUG SUPPRESSORS.

RA PD 315723

Figure 48—Ignition to Battery Wiring Diagram

IGNITION SYSTEM

82. DESCRIPTION.

a. The ignition system differs from that of the conventional automotive types in that it has no distributor. A circuit breaker alone is used. Both coil high-tension winding ends lead directly to both spark plugs. Thus both plugs spark at the same time, one cylinder being on compression stroke while the other cylinder is on exhaust stroke.

83. SPARK PLUGS.

a. Defective spark plugs are indicated by engine missing, overheating, knocking excessively, and lacking normal power.

b. Type. Spark plugs are medium heat range, manufacturer's (H-D) No. 3.

c. Cleaning. Do not take plugs apart for cleaning. Use the sandblast cleaner method.

d. Point Adjustment. Bend electrode located in plug base to adjust point gap 0.025 inch to 0.030 inch.

e. Replacement. Use spark plug wrench (41-W-3334) to install plugs, using new gaskets. Never draw a cool plug up tight in a hot cylinder head, rather turn down snug and wait $\frac{1}{2}$ minute until plug base is warm; then tighten securely. CAUTION: *Take care not to cross-thread when installing spark plug.*

84. CIRCUIT BREAKER POINTS (fig. 49).

a. Circuit breaker lever is insulated from ground and connects to primary wire binding post by means of a "pig-tail" wire. Stationary point is grounded to timer base and is movable in order to adjust circuit breaker points. Circuit breaker points that are burned or pitted should be renewed or dressed with a clean fine-cut, contact-point file. The file should not be used on other metals and should not be allowed to become greasy or dirty. CAUTION: *Never use emery cloth to clean points.* Contact surfaces. after considerable use. may not appear bright and smooth. but this is not necessarily an indication that they are not functioning satisfactorily.

b. Remove Breaker Lever.

(1) To disconnect condenser terminal, remove nut from end of condenser and remove gear-toothed washer, plain washer. and the brass terminal strip. Do not remove fiber washer and plain washer located back of brass terminal strip on condenser terminal post.

ADJUSTABLE POINT
ASSEMBLY

LEVER ASSEMBLY

RAPD 310248

Figure 49—Circuit Breaker Points Removed

(2) Bend brass terminal strip down and remove binding nut which secures brass terminal strip and breaker lever "pig-tail" to primary wire binding post.

(3) Compress breaker lever spring at end of lever, disengaging spring. CAUTION: *Do not lose spring.* Release and remove lever from insulated pivot post.

c. Remove Adjustable Contact Point.

(1) Remove the two lock screws and washer plate, securing adjustable contact point assembly to timer base. Point assembly is free to be lifted off lever pivot stud.

d. Install Adjustable Contact Point.

(1) Install contact point assembly, replacing washer plate and the two lock screws. Do not tighten lock screws until circuit breaker points are adjusted (step f below).

e. Install Breaker Lever.

(1) Install brass terminal strip on primary wire binding post.

(2) Connect end of brass terminal strip to condenser terminal post. Install flat washer, gear-toothed washer, and nut.

(3) Install breaker lever on pivot post insulated bearing.

(4) Install breaker lever spring. Make sure that ends of spring are retained correctly.

(5) NOTE: *Keep breaker lever cam very lightly greased.*

f. Adjusting Circuit Breaker Points (fig. 51).

(1) Correct point gap is 0.022 inch. Circuit breaker point faces must seat squarely against each other. If bent, square up and aline by bending contact plate. Turn timer breaker cam until breaker lever fiber is located on highest point of cam.

(2) With the adjustable point lock screws loose, shift the adjustable point plate to obtain a 0.022-inch gap between the circuit breaker points. Measure gap with an accurate thickness gage before retightening lock screws, and again recheck point gap after tightening the lock screws. NOTE: *Wrong circuit breaker point gap affects ignition timing.*

85. CONDENSER.

a. The condenser is connected in parallel with the circuit breaker points, one of its terminals being grounded (for the adjustable point) to the timer base by means of the mounting screw, the other terminal making connection with the circuit breaker lever (for the lever point) by means of the lever "pig-tail."

b. Remove.

(1) Unlatch circuit breaker cover retainer and remove cover.

(2) Remove nut from end of condenser and remove gear-toothed washer, plain washer, and the brass terminal strip. NOTE: *A small plain washer and a large fiber washer are located behind brass terminal strip.*

(3) Remove screw which secures condenser to timer base. Remove condenser.

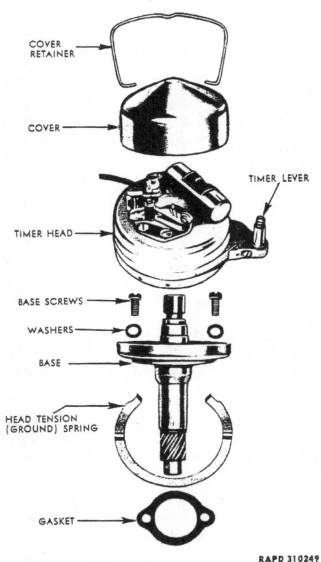

RAPD 310249

Figure 50—Circuit Breaker (Timer), Disassembled

c. **Install.**

(1) Mount condenser on timer housing. Install lock washer and screw. Make sure small plain washer and large fiber washer are in place on condenser end terminal screw before connecting the brass terminal strip.

(2) Connect brass terminal strip to condenser. Replace plain washer, gear-toothed washer and terminal nut.

(3) Install circuit breaker cover.

86. CIRCUIT BREAKER AND TIMER ASSEMBLY (figs. 50 and 51).

a. When the circuit breaker timer shaft and base assembly must be replaced due to excessive wear in timer shaft bearing, sheared worm gear pin, and/or worn or damaged worm gear, engine ignition must be retimed. Ignition timing for the V-type twin engine is difficult and should be attempted only by experienced personnel.

b. **Remove** (fig. 50). Before the timer shaft and base assembly can be removed, the circuit breaker timer head assembly must be removed. NOTE: *If the timer head only, or timer wire, is to be replaced, it is not necessary to remove timer shaft and base assembly, and thus throw engine ignition out of time.*

(1) Remove timer head cover.

(2) Unlatch cover retainer ends from holes in the timer head and remove.

(3) Disconnect spark control wire at timer lever.

(4) Lift the timer head assembly off base. The head seating tension (ground) spring (underneath shaft base) is also free, and can now be removed. NOTE: *It is not necessary to disconnect timer to coil wire from timer head terminal post, unless head or wire is being replaced.*

(5) Remove the two timer base mounting screws and lock washers. It will be noted that one screw grounds the timer to coil wire shielding.

(6) Timer shaft and base assembly can now be lifted out of engine gear case cover. Take care not to damage or misplace base gasket.

c. **Install Timer Shaft and Base Assembly and Timing Ignition** (fig. 51). This calls for retiming engine ignition as follows: (NOTE: *Circuit breaker cam turns in clockwise direction):*

(1) Unscrew and raise front cylinder inlet valve spring cover, using tappet wrench (41-W-3617).

(2) Turn engine in direction in which it runs until valve tappet indicates front cylinder is on compression stroke (directly after front cylinder intake valve closes).

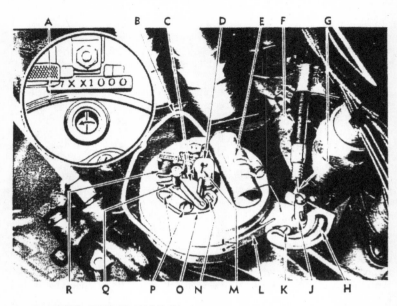

A—FLYWHEEL TIMING MARK IN CRANKCASE INSPECTION HOLE.
B—COVER RETAINER.
C—CIRCUIT BREAKER LEVER.
D—CIRCUIT BREAKER CAM.
E—CONDENSER.
F—SPARK CONTROL WIRE HOUSING
G—SPARK CONTROL WIRE.
H—SPARK LEVER QUADRANT.
J—SPARK LEVER.
K—TIMER HEAD ADJUSTING BAND SCREW.
L—TIMER HEAD ADJUSTING BAND.
M—MARK ON BREAKER CAM AND MARKS ON TIMER HEAD AND HAND INDICATING ORIGINAL FACTORY TIMING.
N—CIRCUIT BREAKER POINTS.
O—ADJUSTABLE CONTACT POINT PLATE.
P—ADJUSTABLE CONTACT POINT LOCK SCREWS.
Q—CIRCUIT BREAKER LEVER PIVOT (INSULATED).
R—BREAKER LEVER SPRING.

RAPD 310281

Figure 51—Circuit Breaker Marks and Flywheel Mark Correctly Alined

(3) Remove plug from timing inspection hole in left-side crankcase.

(4) Continue turning engine slowly until flywheel timing mark is in center of inspection hole (fig. 51). Do not turn engine further.

(5) Install paper gasket and timer head tension (ground) spring on timer shaft base assembly. Make sure bent ends of tension spring are facing downward (away from timer base).

(6) Insert timer shaft and base assembly all the way down into place in timing gear case cover, trying to locate mark on small end

of breaker cam in position shown in figure 51. Do not install base mounting screws as yet.

(7)   Install timer head assembly so that spark control lever is within the advance and retard quadrant (fig. 51). NOTE: *Do not install cover retainer until later.*

(8)   Fully advance spark lever (push inward toward engine) and observe how closely mark on breaker cam lines up with breaker lever fiber. If mark does not line up, lift timer base and turn shaft gear so its engagement with its driving gear is changed one tooth. Check again according to breaker cam mark and breaker lever fiber. Repeat this procedure until gear engagement is obtained which closely alines cam mark and breaker lever fiber.

(9)   See that timer base is turned so that timer to coil wire is toward rear of engine.

(10)   Install timer base screws and lock washers. Make sure that timer to coil wire shielding is grounded under head of screw farthest away from engine (fig. 52). Securely tighten screws.

(11)   Install timer head on base and secure with ground spring and cover retainer. Be sure ground spring is in its proper place so that when cover retainer ends are fitted through holes in the timer head, they will also fit into spring locating notches. It will be necessary to press ground spring upward under timer base to engage retainer ends in the spring notches. NOTE: *If cover retainer ends do not engage ground spring notches, spring will have no tension and timer head will be loose on its base.* Circuit breaker points and condenser are electrically grounded through timer base, and ground spring holds the head and base in close contact, thus assuring a good ground.

(12)   Connect spark control wire and timer lever and adjust (par. 88).

(13)   Engine is now timed according to original factory setting, providing mark on side of timer head and hole in head adjusting band are still in alinement, and circuit breaker point gap is 0.022 inch. Even though all ignition timing marks are in perfect alinement, as outlined in the foregoing instructions, it is advisable to accurately check ignition timing (step d following).

d.   **Recommended Recheck of Ignition Timing** (fig. 51). Even though all ignition timing marks are in perfect alinement, as when engine was originally timed, ignition timing may change somewhat after engine has been in service for a while, due to normal wear and seating of the various moving parts that can affect ignition timing. Since accurate ignition timing is the first essential to good engine performance, it is advisable to check ignition timing on new vehicle after first 1,500 miles of service, and at each 2,000 miles thereafter.

(1) See that circuit breaker points are adjusted for correct gap of 0.022 inch (par. 84 f).

(2) Advance timer lever fully (toward engine).

(3) Turn engine in direction in which it runs until front cylinder is on compression stroke, and continue to turn it ahead slowly until narrow timer cam (the end with the timing mark), just starts to open the circuit breaker points.

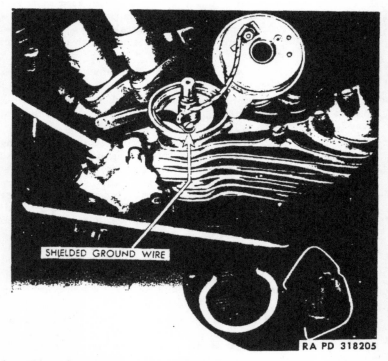

SHIELDED GROUND WIRE

RA PD 318205

Figure 52—Shielding of Coil to Timer Wire Grounded on Base

(4) An accurate test light check as to when points just start to break can be made, using the instrument panel red light for the purpose. Disconnect panel light wire from the oil pressure switch, attaching this wire to the insulated terminal post on timer head. Turn ignition and light switch on. As long as circuit breaker points are closed, lamp will remain lit; as points start to open, lamp will go out. NOTE: *After making use of instrument panel red light for above purpose, reconnect wire to oil pressure switch.*

(5) When exact position is found, where points just start to open, flywheel mark should be in the center of the inspection hole.

(6) If flywheel mark is not in center of hole when points open, readjust ignition timing as necessary (slower or faster) by means of the timer head and band adjustment.

(7) To readjust timer head, loosen adjusting band screw and shift timer head in band. If flywheel timing mark shows forward

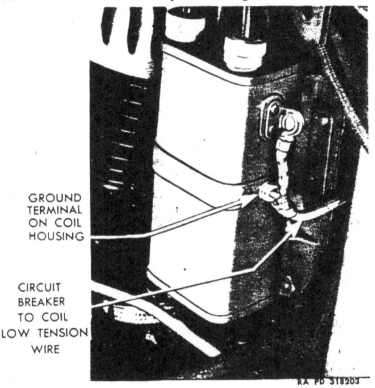

GROUND TERMINAL ON COIL HOUSING

CIRCUIT BREAKER TO COIL LOW TENSION WIRE

RA PD 318203

Figure 53—Shielded Coil to Timer Wire Correctly Connected at Coil

of center in inspection hole, the timing is slow. To correct, shift timer head counterclockwise against rotation of breaker cam. If flywheel mark is to rear of center of inspection hole, timing is fast and timer head must be shifted with rotation (clockwise) of breaker cam, to correct timing.

(8)   With ignition timing correct, front cylinder piston is $\frac{9}{32}$ inch before top dead center, on compression stroke, when circuit breaker points just start to open. At this point spark occurs, igniting front cylinder fuel charge.

(9)   Install flywheel inspection hole plug in left crankcase.

87.   COIL TO TIMER WIRE (figs. 52 and 53).

a.   Models provided with radio shielding are identified by "S" on either side of instrument panel. The coil to timer wire (low-tension wire) on these models is shielded for radio noise suppression.

b.   Remove.

(1)   Disconnect battery negative ground wire at frame connection.

(2)   Remove the two bolts which secure upper end of air cleaner bracket to frame tube. Swing air cleaner and bracket outward and forward to gain access to spark coil rear terminal.

(3)   Disconnect coil to timer wire terminal from coil rear connection. Disconnect wire shielding from coil rear ground connection.

(4)   Refer to paragraph 86 b (1) to (4) for timer head removal.

(5)   Remove timer base mounting screw which secures wire shielding (fig. 52).

(6)   Note position of coil to timer wire inside of timer head; then remove nut washer connecting wire to insulated contact stud.

(7)   Work old wire and loom out of timer head hole and free from vehicle.

(8)   On earlier models, the coil to timer wire was soldered to end of insulated stud. Removal of stud is necessary to remove this wire, or replace it with a shielded wire. Note location of stud insulations on inside and outside of timer head, for correct installation wt reassembling.

c.   Install.

(1)   Pass end of wire, shield terminal, and loom up through hole in timer base.

(2)   Ground the wire shield terminal under head of timer base mounting screw (fig. 52).

(3)   Connect wire end terminal to insulated stud so that wire leads away from stud in direction shown (fig. 52).

(4)   Pass coil to timer wire up alongside and to rear of frame saddle post tube to reach rear of spark coil.

(5)   Ground the wire shield terminal to coil rear ground connection (fig. 53).

(6)   Connect wire terminal to coil rear primary connection (fig. 53).

(7)   Install timer head on base (par. 86 c (11)).

(8)   Connect spark control wire to timer lever and adjust (par. 88).

(9)   Connect battery negative post wire to frame ground terminal.

(10)   Swing air cleaner bracket back into place and install two bolts, washers, and nuts securing bracket to frame clips.

(11)   Replace timer cover and check engine for starting.

88.   ADJUST SPARK CONTROL.

a.   Spark advance and retard is controlled by left handle bar grip. Spark lever operates within a quadrant mounted on engine. Spark must be fully advanced (lever inward toward engine) when handle bar grip is turned inward to full extent of its travel. When handle bar grip is turned outward, spark lever retards (lever outward away from engine).

(1)   With control wire in lever stud and clamp screw loose, turn left grip fully inward; then back it out just a little.

(2)   Shift spark lever inward toward engine as far as it will go: then tighten control wire clamp screw. Test by turning left grip fully inward and noting position of spark lever. It should be against inner side of quadrant (fig. 51). Retard spark and check position of lever within quadrant; it should be against outer side of quadrant.

(3)   Check final adjustment. Readjust full advance and retard timer lever positions as necessary when left grip is turned inward, and outward, respectively.

89.   SPARK COIL (fig. 54).

a.   Spark coil high-tension cables go directly to the spark plugs, no distributor being used. When the coil is faulty, it must be replaced, since internal repairs are not possible. The high-tension cables can be replaced, however. Coil is provided with a condenser for radio noise suppression, and metal coil case is grounded to engine by bonding.

b.   Remove.

(1)   Disconnect battery negative ground wire from frame connection.

(2)   Free high-tension cable ends (with radio noise suppressors) from spark plugs. Free front cylinder high-tension cable from clip at upper engine frame mounting.

(3)   Loosen air intake hose connection at carburetor fitting.

(4)   Remove two nuts, washers, and bolts securing upper end of air cleaner mounting bracket to frame clamps.

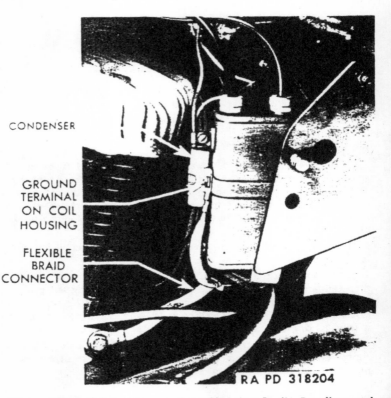

CONDENSER

GROUND
TERMINAL
ON COIL
HOUSING

FLEXIBLE
BRAID
CONNECTOR

RA PD 318204

*Figure 54—Coil Front Connections Showing Radio Bonding and
Noise Suppression Condenser*

(5) Swing air cleaner and bracket assembly outward to gain access to coil rear terminals.

(6) Disconnect coil to timer wire from coil rear terminal screw. Disconnect wire shielding from coil rear ground terminal (fig. 53).

(7) Swing cleaner back and remove wire connections from coil front terminal screw (fig. 54).

(8) Disconnect radio bonding at coil front ground terminal (fig. 54).

(9) Remove nuts and bolts which mount coil to bracket. Coil is now free for removal.

c. Install.

(1) Mount coil on frame bracket with high-tension cables upward, and reinstall mounting bolts, lock washers, and nuts. Tighten nuts.

(2)   Connect terminals of the two green wires to coil front terminal screw. Refer to wiring diagram, figure 48.

(3)   Connect radio bonding to coil front ground terminal. Tighten nut securely.

(4)   Connect coil to timer wire terminal to coil rear terminal screw. Connect wire shielding to coil rear ground terminal. Tighten nut securely.

(5)   Swing air cleaner and bracket assembly back in place and install two bolts, lock washers, and nuts securing bracket to frame clamps. Tighten nuts securely.

(6)   Connect battery negative ground wire to frame connection.

(7)   Pass front cylinder high-tension wire under tank, secure in cable clip at upper engine frame mounting, and attach cable end (radio noise suppressor) to front spark plug. Attach rear high-tension cable end (radio noise suppressor) to rear spark plug.

(8)   Check wiring connections (fig. 48) and test coil by engine starting.

GENERATING SYSTEM

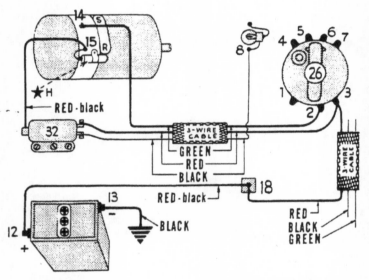

8—GENERATOR SIGNAL LIGHT
12—BATTERY POSITIVE TERMINAL
13—BATTERY NEGATIVE TERMINAL (GROUND)
14—"SWITCH" TERMINAL OF GENERATOR
15—"RELAY" TERMINAL OF GENERATOR

18—FRONT JUNCTION TERMINAL
26—IGNITION AND LIGHT SWITCH
32—CUT-OUT RELAY
•H—NOISE SUPPRESSION CONDENSER
                    RA PD 317200

Figure 55—Generator to Battery Wiring Diagram

90. DESCRIPTION (fig. 55).

a. The generator is shunt connected. The two field coils, regulating coil, and shunt coil are not connected in series in the conventional manner. The regulating field coil provides adequate current output (approx. 4 amperes) for daytime operation. The shunt field coil is controlled through the ignition and light switch to increase current output (approx. 8 amperes) when vehicle lights are in use. Generator uses the third (regulating) brush system of current regulation. A cut-out relay serves as a magnetic switch in the generator-battery circuit, also operating the instrument panel green signal light to indicate generator charge.

COMMUTATOR

GENERATOR END COVER

,RA PD 310259

Figure 56—Generator Cover Removed for Commutator Cleaning

91. CLEAN COMMUTATOR (fig. 56).

a. If battery is in good condition, cut-out relay is functioning, and wiring connections are made according to diagram (fig. 55), yet generator does not charge or charge rate is low, proceed to clean the commutator.

(1) Remove left footboard, sidebar, and clutch foot pedal assembly, following procedure outlined under paragraph 102 a (1) to (6), to permit generator cover removal.

(2)   Remove the two end cover screws and pull end cover off generator.

(3)   Clean armature commutator with No. 00 sandpaper until bright and clean. Blow out with air. CAUTION: *Do not remove or disturb brushes in their holders. Never use emery cloth to clean the commutator.*

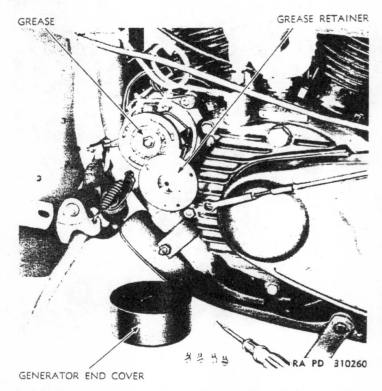

GREASE   GREASE RETAINER

GENERATOR END COVER   RA PD 310260

Figure 57—Generator End Cover and Grease Retainer Removed

(4)   Temporarily install footboard assembly and operate engine, to observe whether or not generator is charging (green signal light goes off at above 20 mph). If cleaning commutator does not remedy generator charge, and/or commutator is badly worn, then generator must be replaced (par. 93). If cleaning of commutator remedied generator charge, reinstall generator end cover, and the footboard and clutch pedal assembly (par. 102 b).

92.   ARMATURE BEARING SPECIAL LUBRICATION (fig. 57).

a.   At the 6,000-mile second echelon preventive maintenance service period, the commutator end bearing must be hand-packed. In performing this operation, care must be taken not to shift or move the generator third (regulating) brush, thus disturbing generator current regulation. Generator drive end bearing is adequately lubricated by oil circulating through engine.

b.   To Lubricate Commutator End Bearing.

(1)   Remove left footboard, sidebar, and clutch pedal assembly, following procedure outlined in paragraph 102 a (1) to (6).

(2)   Remove the two end cover screws and pull end cover off generator.

(3)   Remove two of the three screws which secure the outer grease retainer plate to end of generator (fig. 57).

(4)   Loosen the other grease retainer plate screw slightly to permit shifting plate to one side.

(5)   Pack ball bearing with general purpose grease No. 2, pressing lubricant into bearing with finger.

(6)   Shift the outer grease retainer plate back into position. Install the two screws removed, and securely tighten all three screws.

(7)   Install generator end cover and the two retaining screws.

(8)   Install left footboard, sidebar, and clutch foot pedal assembly, following procedure outlined in paragraph 102 b.

93.   REMOVE GENERATOR (figs. 58 and 59).

a.   Generator is gear driven through engine timing gear train. Generator can be removed and installed without removing timing gear case cover, or affecting alinement of timing gears.

b.   Before replacing generator because of failure of instrument panel green signal light to indicate charge, check panel light wiring and bulb for good condition (par. 120).

c.   When it has been determined that generator must be removed for replacement, proceed as follows:

(1)   Disconnect wires from the two generator terminals marked SWITCH and RELAY.

(2)   Remove the two long screws, through timing gear case cover, that secure end of generator against gear case (fig. 58).

(3)   Remove strap nut, lock washer, and curved washer from end of strap that clamps generator in its cradle on engine crankcase (fig. 59).

(4)   Lift strap high enough to permit raising generator so that oil slinger (on end of generator gear) will clear adjacent gear, and allow generator to be removed from engine. Be sure to observe and

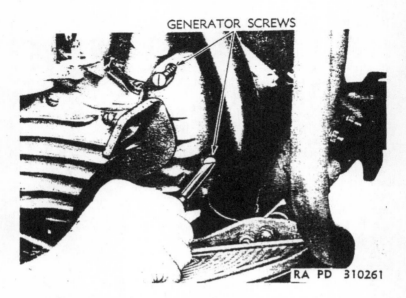

Figure 58—Removing Generator End Mounting Screws

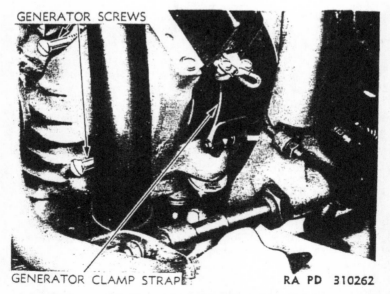

Figure 59—Removing Generator Strap Nut

count number of paper shims between generator and cradle. Lay these shims aside to be used again when generator is reinstalled. Also, note location of hole in shims for oil drain. These shims were required in original assembly to adjust driving gears for proper mesh and, if left out, gears may mesh too deeply and "howl," even though considerably worn. Unless a new generator gasket is available, to be used when generator is reinstalled, be careful not to damage the old one.

94. INSTALL GENERATOR.

a. When installing generator, the important point to consider is correct shimming of generator in its cradle to provide correct mesh of driving gear with intermediate timing gear. Make sure same number of paper shims are used in reassembling as were found underneath generator when it was removed. After an engine has been run a considerable length of time and gears have worn to some extent, they have possibly developed sufficient lash or play to safely remove one or more of the original shims, and thus affect closer meshing and quieter operation. However, this should not be done unless timing gear case cover is removed so that gear mesh and lash can be carefully checked.

(1) Pass generator drive gear end through gear case hole, lifting generator so that oil slinger clears intermediate timing gear. Turn generator in its cradle so that end holes line up with long mounting screws which pass through gear case cover. Tighten mounting screws securely.

(2) Install curved washer, lock washer, and nut on end of clamp strap; tighten nut securely.

(3) Connect red-black wire to generator terminal marked **RE-LAY**, and green wire to generator terminal marked **SWITCH**. Refer to wiring diagram (fig. 55).

(4) Operate engine and check generator for current output, as well as check for gear noise. If shimming under generator is proper, generator and timing gears will run quietly. If necessary, readjust shimming until gears operate quietly.

95. CUT-OUT RELAY.

a. Operation of the instrument panel green signal light, indicating generator charge, is controlled by the cut-out relay. Therefore, if relay is faulty the signal light will not operate properly, falsely indicating generator trouble. Rust around the contact points, burned points, and loss of armature spring tension are sources of most relay trouble. NOTE: *Before condemning a relay because of failure of green signal light, make light test* (par. 120).

b. Correct adjustment of relay point gaps and tensioning of armature springs require use of precision electric meters and expert knowledge on the subject. A faulty relay, other than removing cover and cleaning with air, should be replaced. No adjustment of points should be attempted.

c. **Remove.**

(1)   Disconnect the three wires from relay terminal screws.

(2)   Remove the two mounting screws and lock washers. Remove relay from engine base.

d. **Install.**

(1)   Mount relay on engine base with two screws and lock washers. Make sure that mounting is clean to make good electrical ground contact between relay and engine.

(2)   Reconnect the three wire terminals to relay terminal screws. Follow wiring diagram, figure 55.

(3)   Operate engine and observe action of relay, also action of instrument panel green signal light to indicate generator charge.

Section XX

BRAKE SYSTEM

Paragraph

Rear wheel brake 96

Front wheel brake 97

96. REAR WHEEL BRAKE (figs. 60, 61, and 62).

a. Linkage. Brake foot pedal on right side of vehicle is connected to bell crank (located on rear footboard support rod) by means of the front brake rod (nonadjustable). The bell crank is connected to rear brake operating lever by means of the rear brake rod with adjustable clevis end.

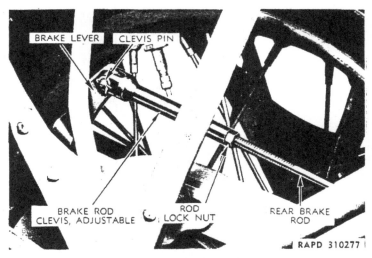

Figure 60—Rear Brake Adjustment

b. Adjusting Rear Wheel Brake (fig. 60). If brake operating lever stands ahead of vertical position, excessive lining wear is indicated. Brake shoes must be replaced (steps c and d below). Normal free play of brake foot pedal before brake operation is 1 inch. After brake takes effect in vehicle operation, brake foot pedal should have 1-inch reserve travel before bottoming on footboard. If brake foot pedal operation does not come within these limits, adjust rear brake rod as follows:

(1)   Remove cotter pin, plain washer, and clevis pin from end of rear brake rod clevis.

(2)   Loosen clevis lock nut on brake rod.

(3) Turn clevis onto (clockwise) brake rod to shorten rod and take up foot pedal free play.

(4) Turn clevis off (counterclockwise) brake rod to lengthen rod and increase foot pedal free play.

(5) After making brake adjustment. spin rear wheel and make sure brake is not dragging. When correct brake adjustment is attained. install clevis pin in clevis and brake operating lever with plain washer. and retain with cotter pin. NOTE: *Cotter pin must be in good condition.*

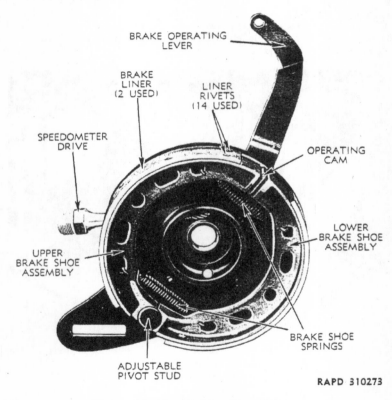

RAPD 310273

Figure 61--Rear Brake Assembly

c. Remove Brake Shoes (fig. 61).

(1) Remove rear wheel (par. 127).

(2) Remove brake drum and sprocket assembly. Brake shoes are now accessible. Do not remove side cover assembly from frame.

(3)   Disconnect brake rod clevis at brake operating lever.

(4)   Place end of large screwdriver blade between ends of brake shoes at pivot stud. Move brake-operating lever forward to hold brake shoes in fully expanded position, and pry ends of shoes off pivot stud without removing brake shoe springs.

d.   **Install Brake Shoes.** Observe that brake shoes are made for upper and lower positions and are not interchangeable. Recess in end of shoe for pivot stud head determines position of shoe in assembly.

(1)   Engage ends of springs in shoe assembly holes from the inside before installing shoes on side cover (fig. 61).

(2)   With brake shoes and springs assembled, install so that ends of shoes will slip over pivot stud and shaft-operating cam.

(3)   Connect brake rod clevis to brake operating lever.

(4)   Install brake drum and sprocket assembly. Lock brake to hold drum in place while installing wheel (fig. 84).

(5)   Install rear wheel (par. 127). NOTE: *If rear chain is in need of adjustment, it should be done at this time.*

(6)   To equalize brake shoes, loosen nut on brake shoe adjustable pivot stud (on outside of brake side plate), and while applying pressure on brake foot pedal (to "center" the brake shoes within the drum), retighten the pivot stud nut.

(7)   After new or relined shoes have been installed, check foot pedal for free play (step b above).

97.   FRONT WHEEL BRAKE (fig. 62).

a.   **Linkage (control).** Handle bar hand lever control wire which operates front wheel brake can be adjusted and/or replaced. Keep brake control wire lubricated (through oiler in housing and at ends of housing) with engine oil.

b.   **Remove Control Wire.** Remove control wire clamp nut from brake lever clevis, and free lower end of control wire from clevis.

(1)   Remove cotter pin and flat washer from hollow pin, permitting hollow pin to be pulled out of hand lever. Control wire can now be pulled out of housing through the hole in hand lever.

c.   **Install Control Wire.** Apply grease or engine oil to new control wire and insert, through hand lever, into control wire housing. Use caution when inserting a new control wire into housing, to prevent wire end from fraying. A frayed wire with loose end strands will not feed through the housing.

(1)   With control wire in housing, insert hand lever hollow pin so that narrow slot straddles control wire; then fit flat washer over end of hollow pin, retaining both with cotter pin.

(2) Insert lower end of control wire through clamp nut. then through clevis and back through clamp nut again. Grasp end of wire with pliers and pull until all slack is taken up. Then. while pulling wire snug, tighten clamp nut securely. Cut off excess wire.

(3) Adjust brake control (refer to step d below).

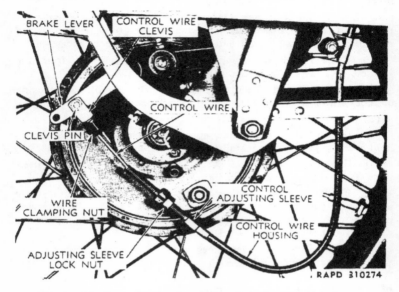

Figure 62—Front Brake Control and Adjusting Members

d. **Adjusting Front Wheel Brake.** End of brake hand lever must move freely about ¼ of its travel before meeting resistance of brake operation.

(1) Loosen adjusting sleeve lock nut and turn adjusting sleeve as necessary to attain correct free movement of hand lever.

(2) After correct hand lever adjustment is made. tighten adjusting sleeve lock nut.

e. **Remove Brake Shoes.**

(1) Remove front wheel (par. 125). After front wheel is removed. brake side cover and shoe assembly is accessible for shoe replacement.

(2) Remove brake shoes. Brake shoes and springs can be pried off pivot stud and freed from operating cam without removing springs.

f. **Install Brake Shoes.** Observe that brake shoes are made for upper and lower positions and are not interchangeable. Recess in end of shoe for pivot stud head determines position of shoe in assembly.

(1)   Engage ends of springs in shoe holes from the inside before installing shoes in brake side plate.

(2)   With shoes and springs assembled, install the shoes so that ends of shoes will slip over pivot stud and shaft operating cam.

(3)   Install front wheel and brake assembly (par. 125).

(4)   Loosen nut on brake shoe adjustable pivot stud and while applying pressure on brake hand lever, retighten pivot stud nut. This is to center brake shoes within the brake drum.

(5)   After new or relined shoes have been installed, check brake hand lever and, if necessary, adjust the control wire (step **d** above).

STEERING CONTROL

98. FORKS (figs. 63 and 64).

a. Either the spring fork can be removed and replaced, or the complete fork assembly (spring fork and rigid) can be replaced.

b. Remove Spring Fork (fig. 63).

(1) Support vehicle on rear stand.

(2) Remove the fork spring rod lock nuts (acorn-type).

(3) Sit on front mudguard, or otherwise provide weight, to compress fork cushion (lower) springs. The spring rod large nuts can then be easily removed, freeing the upper recoil and upper bumper springs for removal.

(4) Remove front wheel (par. 125).

(5) Remove front mudguard (par. 104).

(6) Remove spring fork right and left side rocker plate studs. NOTE: *Leave rigid fork rocker studs, with rockers, attached.*

(7) Remove spring fork from vehicle.

c. Install Spring Fork.

(1) Place buffer springs and lower cushion springs on fork rods. Apply grease to rods. Pass fork rods up through rigid fork bracket. Bind lower end of spring fork to lower end of rigid fork with a strap or piece of heavy wire (fig. 64), to prevent forks from separating while compressing cushion springs.

(2) Install two bolts in the rigid fork brackets which mount the mudguard; then place a rod about 8 inches long on the brackets to provide a pry base for the leverage bar when compressing cushion springs (fig. 64). With a leverage bar about 18 inches long, anchored on top of the pry base rod and under the spring fork, lift upward to compress cushion springs sufficiently to install one of the rocker plates. Then install the other rocker plate (fig. 64). NOTE: *Left side spring fork rocker plate stud has a button end which fits into notch in brake stabilizer plate.*

(3) Install mudguard (par. 104).

(4) Install front wheel (par. 125).

(5)   Install the two spring rod bushings. Install upper bumper springs and upper recoil springs on the fork rods, applying grease to rods.

(6)   Remove blocks from under vehicle.

(7)   Sit on mudguard to compress fork cushion (lower) springs. Tighten the two large spring rod nuts sufficiently to provide full thread for the spring rod lock nuts (acorn-type). Install spring rod lock nuts and tighten.

(8)   See that all nuts, bolts, and screws securing lamp bracket, mudguard, scabbard carrier, and ammunition carrier are tightened securely.

(9)   Check front wheel brake for operation.

d.   **Remove Upper Recoil Springs and/or Upper Bumper Springs.**

(1)   Support vehicle on rear stand. Remove the fork spring rod lock nuts (acorn-type).

(2)   Sit on front mudguard, or otherwise provide weight, to compress fork cushion (lower) springs. The spring rod large nuts can then be easily removed, freeing the upper recoil and upper bumper springs for removal.

e.   **Install Upper Recoil Springs and/or Upper Bumper Springs.**

(1)   Apply grease to fork spring rods and install upper bumper springs.

(2)   Install upper recoil springs over bumper springs on fork spring rods.

(3)   Sit on front mudguard to compress cushion (lower) springs sufficiently to start on spring rod large nuts.

(4)   Tighten both spring rod large nuts. Install and tighten the two spring rod (acorn-type) lock nuts.

f.   **Remove and Install Lower Cushion Springs and/or Lower Buffer Springs.** This operation calls for same procedure followed in removing and installing spring fork (steps b and c above).

g.   **Remove Complete Fork Assembly.**

(1)   Remove ammunition box carrier (par. 103).

(2)   Remove scabbard carrier (par. 103).

(3)   Remove front wheel (par. 125).

(4)   Remove steering damper (par. 99).

(5)   Remove front mudguard, after removing nuts and locks from rear rocker plate studs, two screws and nuts securing mudguard to rigid fork, and the two bolts mounting headlight bracket to mudguard. NOTE: *Front mudguard blackout light wire connects to*

Figure 63—Spring Fork Disassembled

RA PD 315728

A—UPPER (RECOIL) SPRINGS

B—UPPER BUMPER SPRINGS

C—SPRING ROD LOCK NUTS (ACORN-TYPE)

D—SPRING ROD BUSHINGS

E—LARGE SPRING ROD NUTS

F—LOWER CUSHION SPRINGS

G—SPRING RODS

H—LOWER BUFFER SPRINGS

J—SPRING FORK ASSEMBLY

K—-ROCKER PLATE STUD NUTS AND LOCKS

L—RIGHT SIDE ROCKER PLATE STUD AND WASHER

M—LEFT SIDE ROCKER PLATE STUD (HAS BUTTON END) AND WASHER

N—AMMUNITION BOX CARRIER MOUNTING BOLT, WASHERS AND NUT

O—HEADLIGHT BRACKET AND MUDGUARD BOLT, WASHER AND NUT
(LEFT SIDE)

P—FRONT AXLE, CASTLE NUT AND COTTER PIN

Q—SCABBARD CARRIER MOUNTING BOLT, WASHERS AND NUT

R—-HEADLIGHT BRACKET AND MUDGUARD BOLT, MARKER LIGHT CABLE
CLIP, WASHER AND NUT (RIGHT SIDE)

S—BRAKE SHACKLE BOLT, LOCK AND NUT

T—-BRAKE AND SIDE COVER ASSEMBLY

U—-MUDGUARD BRACKET MOUNTING LOCK, WASHER AND NUTS (RIGHT
SIDE)

V—MUDGUARD AND RIGID FORK MOUNTING SCREWS, WASHERS AND
NUTS

W—MUDGUARD BRACKET MOUNTING LOCK, WASHER AND NUTS (LEFT
SIDE)

X—NOTCHES IN MUDGUARD BRACKETS FOR SPECIAL LOCKS

RA PD 315728B

Legend for Figure 63—Spring Fork Disassembled

*ignition and light switch and care must be exercised not to break
this wire if it is not disconnected from the switch.*

(6) Disconnect battery negative ground wire at frame connection. Remove blackout light (par. 114). Remove headlight, horn, and bracket assembly as one unit.

(7) Remove handle bar brake fittings and brake control wire housing from side of fork. Remove handle bars after removing handle bar bracket lock nut and cone lock plate. It is not necessary to disconnect spark and throttle control wire housings from frame. Unscrew fork upper adjusting cone from fork stem, freeing fork assembly to be removed from frame head. NOTE: *Steering head ball bearings are loose (not in retainers) in upper and lower frame head bearing cups. Take care not to lose balls.*

h. **Install Fork Assembly.** With vehicle on rear stand, and front end up by blocking under frame loop or skid plate, proceed with installing fork assembly, as follows:

(1) Thoroughly clean upper and lower frame head bearing cups and pack with general purpose grease No. 2, installing fifteen $\frac{5}{16}$-inch ball bearings in each cup. Work grease thoroughly in between balls.

(2) See that lower fork stem cone is clean and in place, pass fork stem up through frame head, turning on upper adjusting cone. Do not try to adjust bearing cone as yet.

(3) Install handle bars by locating mounting bracket on ends of fork sides and center stem, making sure that spark and throttle control wire housings are in place.

(4) Adjust upper fork stem adjusting cone so that there is no perceptible shake in head bearings when handle bars are worked up and down, and fork does not bind when turned to right and left extremes.

(5) Install cone lock plate by engaging pin in one of the cone notches.

(6) Install lock nut on stem and tighten securely. NOTE: *Check head bearing play, as tightening lock nut sometimes makes head bearing too tight. Readjust if necessary.*

(7) Attach handle bar brake fittings and brake control wire housing to side of fork.

(8) Reinstall headlight, horn, and bracket assembly. Connect wires (per wiring diagram fig. 73) before front mudguard is reinstalled. Install blackout light (par. 114). Reconnect battery negative ground wire to frame ground connection.

(9) Install steering damper (par. 99).

(10) Install front mudguard. Attach two screws, washers, and nuts for rigid fork mounting and two bolts, washers, and nuts for

BAR   PRY BAR

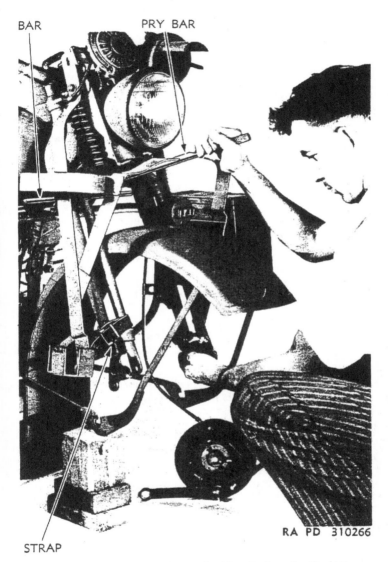

STRAP

RA PD 310266

Figure 64—Compressing Cushion Springs for Spring Fork Assembly

headlight bracket mounting. Fit right and left mudguard brace clip locks to right and left side rocker plate studs respectively. Do not put on nuts until after installing ammunition box carrier and scabbard carrier.

(11)   Install front wheel (par. 125).

(12)   Install scabbard carrier and ammunition box carrier (par. 103).

(13)   Check lights, horn, spark control, throttle control, front brake control, steering damper control, and steering head bearing for freedom without binding.

i.   **Remove Rocker Plate Studs.** Studs and/or rocker plates can be removed and installed in the same operation. In removing and installing studs, remove only one fork rocker plate at a time, leaving the other plate attached to opposite side fork ends to hold fork springs in compressed position. This will eliminate necessity of compressing fork springs to fit rocker plates on studs.

(1)   Remove front wheel (par. 125).

(2)   Remove nuts and locks from rocker plate studs on right side of vehicle. This releases gun scabbard carrier and mudguard stay clip. NOTE: *Remove the large nut which secures the long stud to rigid fork.*

(3)   Drive out studs from fork ends, releasing rocker plate.

(4)   Install studs and rocker plate before removing studs from left side of vehicle.

j.   **Install Rocker Plate Studs.** Apply grease to studs and insert in rocker plate, then install large flat washers on studs before mounting this assembly on fork ends. Make sure that short stud is in front position, and that long stud is in rear position for the rigid fork.

(1)   Drift studs (with plate assembly) into fork end holes from the inside.

(2)   Install special nut lock (with half round hole) on front stud and turn stud as necessary to make lock "cup" over end of fork. Install and tighten stud nut and bend up end of lock for security. Place lock washer over long stud and install thick nut, securely tightening it.

(3)   Attach end of gun scabbard carrier and mudguard brace clip with special lock to long stud, replacing washer and nut.

(4)   After right side rocker plate and/or studs have been installed, remove and install studs and/or plate on left side of vehicle following same step-by-step procedure as above. The exceptions will be ammunition box carrier instead of scabbard carrier; also, the left side front stud is special, having a "button" end.

(5)   Install front wheel (par. 125).

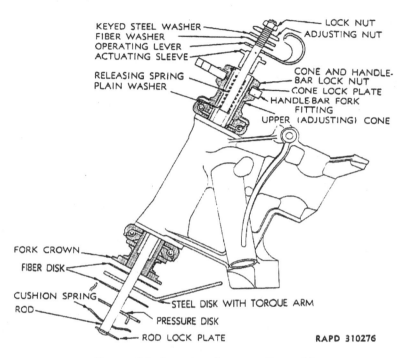

KEYED STEEL WASHER
FIBER WASHER
OPERATING LEVER
ACTUATING SLEEVE
RELEASING SPRING
PLAIN WASHER
LOCK NUT
ADJUSTING NUT
CONE AND HANDLE-BAR LOCK NUT
CONE LOCK PLATE
HANDLE-BAR FORK FITTING
UPPER (ADJUSTING) CONE
FORK CROWN
FIBER DISK
CUSHION SPRING
ROD
STEEL DISK WITH TORQUE ARM
PRESSURE DISK
ROD LOCK PLATE
RAPD 310276

Figure 65—Steering Damper Assembly

99. STEERING DAMPER (fig. 65).

a. Remove (fig. 65).

(1)   Remove front wheel (par. 125).

(2)   Remove front mudguard (par. 104).

(3)   Remove lock nut from steering damper rod, then remove upper end parts in the following order: adjusting nut, keyed steel washer, fiber washer, operating lever, and actuating sleeve. This entire assembly is located in the central part of the handle bar mounting bracket.

(4)   Steering damper rod, cushion spring, pressure disk, fiber disk, and steel disk assembly can now be withdrawn (downward) from fork stem hole.

b. Install (fig. 65). Before installing steering damper, make sure that the parts are in correct order on the lower end of the rod before passing rod up through hole in fork stem. Check parts and order of assembly.

(1)   Assemble parts on rod end (fig. 65), making sure that the bent down lip of the steel pressure disk engages with notch in end of the rod lock plate.

(2)   Pass rod with its lower end assembly up through hole in fork stem, turning steel pressure disk to front position so that "bent-up" lip engages with notch in front side of rigid fork crown, at the same time engaging curved end of steel disk torque arm in slot in underside of frame head. Maintain pressure against end of rod to keep lower disks in order while assembling upper rod end parts.

(3)   Install upper rod end assembly in the following order: Small plain washer, releasing spring, adjusting sleeve screws into end of fork stem, operating lever registers on the adjusting sleeve, fiber washer, keyed steel washer registers in rod slot, large adjusting nut, and lock nut.

(4)   Turn actuating sleeve all the way into fork stem and then back it out (up) $\frac{1}{2}$ turn or more. Register the operating lever on flat of actuating sleeve, and see that lever has full movement to the left without bottoming sleeve in the fork stem.

(5)   Adjust steering damper by setting adjusting (large) nut so that operating lever must be moved nearly straight back from the free (left-side) position, before damper takes noticeable effect (applies friction to movement of the handle bars). Hold large adjusting nut and tighten the small lock nut.

(6)   Install front mudguard (par. 104).

(7)   Install front wheel (par. 125).

100.   HANDLE BARS.

a.   **Remove Complete Assembly.** If vehicle is equipped with handle bar windshield and rear view mirror, remove these accessories before starting to remove handle bar assembly.

(1)   Disconnect throttle control wire at carburetor lever, and spark control wire at timer lever.

(2)   Release spark control wire housing clip at front cylinder base bolt (near timer). Also release housing from frame clip on left side of vehicle. Release throttle control wire housing clip, located at tank, lower front connection bolt.

(3)   Remove front brake hand lever fittings from handle bars. Also release brake control wire housing at handle bar clamp.

(4)   Disconnect battery negative ground wire at frame connection and wires at headlight. Headlight must be removed for access to the two terminal screws (fig. 73).

(5)   Disconnect horn wire leading to handle bars and red wire (terminal No. 17, fig. 73) leading to handle bars.

(6)   Remove steering damper rod upper end fittings in the following order: Lock nut, adjusting nut, keyed steel washer, fiber washer, operating lever, and operating sleeve (screws into end of fork stem). Removal of these parts gives access to handle bar lock nut. Remove handle bar lock nut and cone lock plate.

(7)   Loosen handle bar bracket-fork end pinch bolts. Handle bars are now free to be drifted off ends of fork sides and center stem.

(8)   Remove handle bar windshield apron spring guard after handle bars are removed from vehicle.

b.   **Install Complete Assembly.** If vehicle is equipped with handle bar windshield and rear view mirror, attach these accessories after handle bar assembly is installed.

(1)   Attach windshield apron spring guard to handle bar bracket. Do not tighten bolt nut until after handle bars are installed.

(2)   Start handle bar bracket holes over ends of fork, seeing that spark control wire housing is on right side of frame head: then drive handle bars onto fork ends, using a rawhide mallet, or a hammer and wood block.

(3)   To install cone lock plate, enter registering pin through hole in handle bars and engage notch in the adjusting cone. Install and tighten handle bar lock nut securely. CAUTION: *When tightening this nut, always make sure that register (shoulder) of nut enters hole in lock plate and handle bars.*

(4)   Check adjustment of head bearing. The fork must turn freely b it without perceptible shake. Readjust head cone to obtain proper bearing adjustment if necessary.

(5)   Tighten handle bar bracket-fork end pinch bolts.

(6)   Position windshield apron guard so that it clears fork springs. Securely tighten mounting bolt nut.

(7)   Install steering damper upper end fittings (fig. 65). Make sure that lower end disks and plates are properly engaged. Adjust (par. 99).

(8)   Connect handle bar wires to terminal plate, horn, and headlight. Consult wiring diagram (fig. 73). Install headlight. Adjust beam and secure mounting nut (par. 114). Connect battery negative ground wire to frame connection.

(9)   Check operation of lights and horn, tactical situation permitting.

(10)   Attach front brake hand lever fittings to left handle bar. Secure control wire housing in handle bar clamp, just ahead of housing oiler. Check front brake for correct operation and, if necessary, adjust (par. 97).

(11)   Pass spark control wire housing along left side of frame front tube, between cylinders (under carburetor) to position housing

end clamp on cylinder stud near timer. Secure clamp under cylinder stud nut. Secure wire cable under clamp on left side of frame front tube, with white paint mark slightly ahead of clamp front edge. Engage end of spark control wire in timer lever and adjust spark control (par. 88).

(12) Pass throttle control wire housing along right side of frame front tube and over top of front cylinder head to reach carburetor connection. Install tank (lower front) mounting bolt to secure wire housing clamp. See that white paint mark on wire housing is slightly ahead of clamp, then secure bolt nut on left side of vehicle. Engage end of throttle control wire in throttle lever and adjust (par. 69).

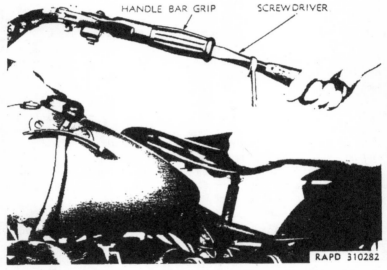

Figure 66—Removing Handle Bar Grip Sleeve Retaining Nut

101. HANDLE BAR CONTROLS (figs. 66 and 67).

a. Construction of the throttle and spark controls is the same, thus replacing a control wire or wire housing follows the same general procedure up to the point where control adjustment is made. Handle bar grip sleeves (spirals) are interchangeable.

b. **Remove Throttle Control Wire** (fig. 67).

(1) Disconnect control wire at throttle lever connection.

(2) Insert blade of a large, square-shank screwdriver through hole in end of grip and turn out end nut by using a wrench on the shank of the screwdriver (fig. 66). Sometimes this nut is difficult to remove. In this case, insert punch into the slot in the nut and

strike punch two or three sharp blows to "free" nut in handle bar
end threads. Remove nut as above. NOTE: *Nut remains inside the
grip and is removed with the grip and spiral sleeve assembly.*

(3)   Remove grip and spiral assembly from handle bars. Control
wire and working parts are now accessible.

(4)   Remove plain roller from pin. Remove roller block from pin.
Remove pin from plunger.

(5)   Pull plunger with wire attached out of handle bar end. Remove hexagon head screw which secures wire to plunger. NOTE: *If
wire is broken, remove other half from housing at carburetor connection end.*

(6)   Remove any rust, dirt, or gum from grip spiral, handle bar
end, wire plunger, and inside of handle bar where plunger operates.

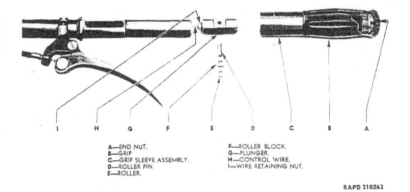

A—END NUT.
B—GRIP
C—GRIP SLEEVE ASSEMBLY.
D—ROLLER PIN.
E—ROLLER.

F—ROLLER BLOCK.
G—PLUNGER.
H—CONTROL WIRE.
I—WIRE RETAINING NUT.

RAPD 310263

Figure 67—Handle Bar Grip and Wire Control, Disassembled

c.   Install Throttle Control Wire (fig. 67).

(1)   Pass hollow screw over control wire with threaded end of
hollow screw facing button on end of wire. Install screw in end of
plunger. Securely tighten screw.

(2)   Apply grease or engine oil to control wire and insert end into
control wire housing.

(3)   Apply grease to plunger and push plunger and wire into
handle bar until plunger pin hole is exposed in handle bar slot. Work
plunger or turn it within handle bar so that pin hole and flat side
are upward and are centered in slot; then insert roller pin into
plunger hole, roller block (with flat sides), and roller in order named.
Apply grease to plunger pin and roller and to outside of handle bar
end.

(4)   Install grip and spiral assembly by engaging plunger roller in spiral opening in end of grip sleeve. Grip spiral sleeve nut can best be started without danger of cross threading, by holding grip assembly back slightly while starting nut in handle bar end. This squares nut with end of grip sleeve, alining threads. Securely tighten nut with screwdriver and wrench.

(5)   Connect control wire at throttle lever connection. Adjust control (par. 69).

d.   **Remove Spark Control Wire** (fig. 67). Disconnect control wire at timer lever and follow procedure outlined under step **b** above.

e.   **Install Spark Control Wire** (fig. 67). Follow procedure outlined under step **c** above, then connect control wire at timer lever and adjust control (par. 88).

f.   **Remove and Install Control Wire Housings.** Remove either control wire housing after following procedure outlined above (step **b**), then remove set screw on under side of handle bar, just ahead of grip sleeve shoulder. NOTE: *Set screw for spark control wire housing is located under headlight dimmer switch.* After set screw is removed and housing freed from attaching clamps, housing can be pushed out through end of handle bar.

(1)   When installing control wire housings, see that housing end is secured in handle bar with set screw, and that housing is correctly attached to vehicle clamps.

(2)   Install control wire and grip (step **c** above) and adjust controls: spark (par. 88), throttle (par. 69).

SHEET METAL AND EQUIPMENT

102. CHAIN GUARDS.

   a. Remove Outer Front Chain Guard (figs. 68 and 69).

   (1) Remove nut and washer which secures center of chain guard and skid plate left-side support bracket.

   (2) Loosen skid plate support bracket lower bolt and nut and remove bracket from stud.

   (3) Loosen the nut which secures footboard rear stud to sidebar, then remove nut which secures footboard front stud to sidebar. Pull front end of footboard away from sidebar so that stud will clear end of safety guard.

   (4) Remove extended nut which secures sidebar to frame front support rod.

   (5) Disconnect clutch control cable end at clutch foot pedal by removing cotter pin and plain washer from stud.

   (6) Left side footboard, sidebar, and clutch foot pedal assembly can now be removed. If rear end of sidebar is lowered, the front end will clear end of safety guard.

   (7) Remove cotter pin, nut, spring, washer, and bolt from chain guard rear mounting. Outer front chain guard can now be removed, exposing engine sprocket, front drive chain, and clutch assembly.

   b. Install Outer Front Chain Guard.

   (1) Locate outer front chain guard on center support stud (frame rear support rod end). Line up rear mounting bracket with frame bracket.

   (2) Install bolt, washer, spring, nut, and cotter pin to secure rear mounting.

   (3) Install footboard, sidebar, and clutch foot pedal assembly on frame support rod ends.

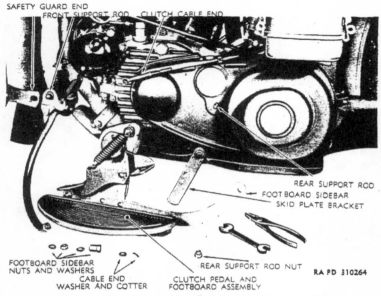

SAFETY GUARD END
FRONT SUPPORT ROD   CLUTCH CABLE END

REAR SUPPORT ROD
FOOT BOARD SIDEBAR
SKID PLATE BRACKET

FOOTBOARD SIDEBAR
NUTS AND WASHERS

CABLE END
WASHER AND COTTER

REAR SUPPORT ROD NUT

CLUTCH PEDAL AND
FOOTBOARD ASSEMBLY

RA PD 310264

Figure 68—Left Footboard Assembly Removed

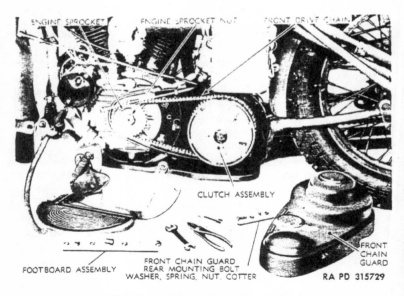

ENGINE SPROCKET   ENGINE SPROCKET NUT   FRONT DRIVE CHAIN

CLUTCH ASSEMBLY

FOOTBOARD ASSEMBLY

FRONT CHAIN GUARD
REAR MOUNTING BOLT
WASHER, SPRING, NUT, COTTER

FRONT
CHAIN
GUARD

RA PD 315729

Figure 69—Outer Front Chain Guard Removed

(4)   Attach front end of sidebar. Install extended nut and lock washer to secure front sidebar and support rod mounting.

(5)   Install skid plate support bracket on support rod (in center of chain guard), tightening nut on bolt. Install nut and lock washer which secure skid plate bracket and chain guard on rear support rod. Tighten nut.

(6)   Pull front end of footboard away from sidebar so that hole in end of safety guard lines up with hole in sidebar, then pass footboard stud through both pieces, installing washer and securing stud nut. Tighten footboard rear stud nut.

(7)   Attach brake control cable end to foot pedal stud.

c.   Remove Rear Chain Guard.

(1)   Remove cap screw which secures rear chain oil pipe clamp, and provides mounting for front end of chain guard on transmission sprocket cover. Remove chain guard.

(2)   Remove chain guard from rear mounting by pushing the guard back so that stud (with washers and spring) slips out of mounting clip notch.

d.   Install Rear Chain Guard.

(1)   Locate rear chain guard in position for mounting. Spread the large washer on the rear stud to engage clip notch. Push guard forward until front end hole lines up with chain oiler pipe clamp, then install cap screw and washer, securing guard and clip to sprocket cover.

103.   CARRIERS.

a.   Remove Ammunition Box Carrier.

(1)   Remove nut and screw which secures carrier bracket to front mudguard.

(2)   Remove nut and lock washer from rocker plate rear stud. This frees lower end of carrier.

(3)   Remove nut, washer, cable clip, and plain washer from rigid fork stud. Remove carrier and box.

b.   Install Ammunition Box Carrier.

(1)   Locate hole in lower end of bracket on rocker plate rear stud. Attach upper end of bracket to rigid fork stud. Replace lock washers and nuts. Tighten nuts.

(2)   Attach carrier bracket to front mudguard with screw, washer, and nut. Tighten nut.

c.   Remove and Install Scabbard Carrier. The procedure for removing and installing scabbard carrier is the same as outlined for ammunition box carrier, except that scabbard carrier is on left side of vehicle. Follow procedure outlined under steps **a** and **b** above.

d. Remove Luggage Carrier.

(1) Loosen straps of both saddlebags, and remove saddlebags from keyhole notches in luggage carrier side plates. Remove nuts from right and left side mounting studs, which secure luggage carrier to frame clips. Deflate rear wheel tire so that a piece of wood or suitable object can be used to depress top part of tire under mudguard, to provide clearance, and access to the three nuts which secure screws for luggage carrier mudguard mounting. NOTE: *If rear wheel is removed, mounting screws are accessible.*

(2) Remove the three luggage carrier center mounting screws. Remove luggage carrier from vehicle.

e. Install Luggage Carrier.

(1) Mount luggage carrier on frame clip studs. Install washers and nuts. With rear tire deflated and depressed for clearance under mudguard, install the three screws, lock washers, and nuts for carrier-mudguard mounting. NOTE: *If rear wheel is removed, mounting screws are accessible.*

(2) Tighten frame stud nuts to secure both sides of carrier.

(3) Attach saddlebags and securely strap to frame stays.

(4) Inflate tire to 20 pounds.

104. MUDGUARDS.

a. Remove Front Mudguard.

(1) Remove front wheel (par. 125).

(2) Remove instrument panel cover (par. 119). disconnect front mudguard blackout marker light wire at switch. Pull wire out, free from tanks.

(3) Remove the two screws and nuts from rigid fork and mudguard mounting. Remove the two screws and nuts securing lamp bracket to mudguard.

(4) Remove bolt and nut which secure ammunition box carrier to mudguard.

(5) Remove bolt and nut which secure gun scabbard carrier to mudguard.

(6) Remove nuts from fork left rocker plate stud. These nuts secure ammunition box lower bracket. and mudguard stay clip. Remove nuts from fork right rocker plate stud. These nuts secure gun scabbard carrier lower bracket. and mudguard stay clip.

(7) Pull carrier brackets off rocker plate studs. Remove mudguard brace clip locks from slots in clips so that mudguard can be dropped. When removing mudguard from vehicle, take care not to break and/or damage blackout light wire.

b. Install Front Mudguard.

(1)   Locate mudguard in mounting position. Engage slots in stay clips on rocker plate studs, installing the special locks in the clip slots. NOTE: *Brace clip locks are made for right and left side installation. Secure both clip locks with stud nuts.*

(2)   Attach ends of ammunition and scabbard carriers to rocker plate studs. Secure with lock washers and nuts.

(3)   Mount mudguard to rigid fork bracket. Tighten the two screws, washers, and nuts.

(4)   Attach lower end of headlight bracket to mudguard with two bolts, washers, and nuts.

(5)   Attach ammunition box carrier bracket to mudguard. Tighten bolt, washer, and nut.

(6)   Attach gun scabbard carrier bracket to mudguard. Tighten bolt, washer, and nut.

(7)   Reinstall front wheel and brake assembly (par. 125).

(8)   Connect mudguard blackout light wire to switch terminal. Refer to wiring diagram, figure 73.

(9)   Install instrument panel cover (par. 119).

c. Remove Rear Mudguard.

(1)   Support vehicle on rear stand. Remove rear wheel (par. 127).

(2)   Remove luggage carrier (par. 103).

(3)   Remove rear chain guard (par. 102).

(4)   Remove the two U-bolt nuts which mount safety guard at upper frame bracket. Then pull safety guard away from studs and remove studs from frame bracket, freeing mudguard at this point. NOTE: *These two studs screw into a "plate" nut.*

(5)   Remove bolt and nut which secure battery box left-side bracket to mudguard.

(6)   Remove bolt and nut which secure battery box right-side bracket. This bolt also secures lower tool box bracket and speedometer cable clip to mudguard.

(7)   Remove nut and washers from bolt which secures lower end of mudguard to frame (behind transmission).

(8)   Remove taillight connector plugs from sockets and remove cable from mudguard spring clips.

(9)   Remove nuts from studs which secure right- and left-side mudguard brace clips to frame axle clips. Mudguard can now be removed from vehicle.

d. Install Rear Mudguard.

(1)   Locate mudguard in position for mounting. Install the two studs, washers, and nuts which secure right- and left-side brace clips

to frame axle clips. NOTE: *If brake side cover interferes with locating nut on right side, loosen the brake sleeve nut and push brake side cover assembly inward for clearance. Be sure to retighten brake sleeve nut.*

(2)   Attach front lower end of mudguard. Install flat washer, lock washer, and nut on bolt to secure lower end of mudguard to frame (in back of transmission).

(3)   Install the two studs which mount mudguard and upper battery box bracket on frame bracket. These two studs screw into a plate nut located underneath the battery box bracket. Removing the battery box cover will give more access to plate nut in this step. Install battery box cover if it is removed for this job.

(4)   Attach rear safety guard to the two frame bracket studs. Install washers and nuts. Securely tighten nuts and tighten U-bolt nuts, which secure ends of safety guard to frame stays.

(5)   Attach battery box bracket to mudguard bracket. Install bolt, washer, and nut which secure battery box right-side bracket, tool box bracket lower end, and speedometer cable clip to mudguard bracket. Bolt is inserted from front side, head toward engine. NOTE: *Speedometer cable clip is under head of bolt.*

(6)   Attach left-side mudguard bracket and battery box bracket. Install bolt, washer, and nut which secure battery box left-side bracket to mudguard bracket. Bolt is inserted from front side, head toward engine.

(7)   Install rear chain guard (par. 102).

(8)   Locate and retain taillight cable in mudguard spring clips. Attach connector plugs to taillights (wiring diagram, fig. 73).

(9)   Install luggage carrier (par. 103).

(10)   Install rear wheel (par. 127).

(11)   Securely tighten all bolts and nuts.

105.   BATTERY BOX.

a.   Remove Battery Box.

(1)   Remove battery (par. 113).

(2)   To remove rear brake rod, disconnect clevis from brake lever, and free front end of rod at brake shaft bell crank.

(3)   Remove rear chain guard (par. 102).

(4)   Remove tool box and bracket in one piece (par. 106).

(5)   Remove nut and bolt securing left side lower battery box mounting to mudguard bracket. Remove nut and bolt securing battery front mounting to frame saddle post tube bracket.

(6)   Remove the two nuts securing rear safety guard center connection to mounting studs. Unscrew mounting studs to free the plate nut which clamps the battery box bracket to frame cross member.

(7)   Remove battery box from right side of vehicle.

b.   Install Battery Box. Locate battery box in vehicle from left side and secure upper rear mounting bracket with the two frame cross member studs and the plate nut. Install washers and nuts which secure safety guard to these same two studs.

(1)   Install bolt to secure battery box front mounting to frame tube. Make sure that bolt passes through frame tube bracket from left side, and that large plain washer bears against battery box front bracket (bracket has open end). Tighten nut to secure box bracket to frame tube bracket.

(2)   Install tool box and bracket (par. 106).

(3)   Install bolt, washer, and nut which secure battery box left-side mounting to mudguard. Insert bolt from the front.

(4)   Install rear chain guard (par. 102).

(5)   Connect rear brake rod end to bell crank fitting. Attach clevis to brake operating lever, installing plain washer, clevis pin, and cotter pin.

(6)   Install battery (par. 113).

106. TOOL BOX.

a.   General. When tool box only is to be removed and/or installed, it is a simple matter to open box and remove and/or install the three large screws. Gear-toothed lock washers and large recessed washers fit under screw heads.

b.   Remove Box and Bracket Assembly. Remove bolt and nut which secure tool box upper mounting bracket to frame clip. Lower end of mounting bracket, battery box bracket, and speedometer cable are all secured to the mudguard bracket by the same bolt and nut. Remove speedometer cable from clip and remove bolt and nut, freeing tool box and bracket assembly for removal. NOTE: *Removal of rear brake rod will make bracket lower mounting bolt and nut more accessible.*

c.   Install Box and Bracket Assembly. Locate box and bracket assembly on vehicle and install bolt, washer, and nut at the upper frame clip mounting. To attach bracket lower end to mudguard bracket, place bolt through speedometer cable clip, then through box mounting bracket, battery box bracket, and mudguard bracket, securing assembly with lock washer and nut.

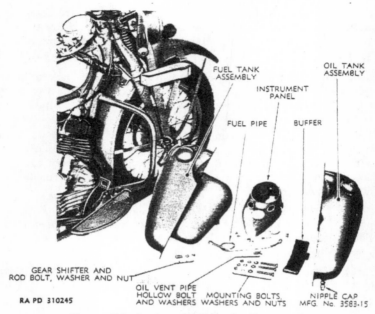

RA PD 310245

Figure 70—Fuel and Oil Tanks Removed

107. TANKS (fig. 70).

a. **General.** Fuel and oil tanks are separate, fitting together, saddle-type, in upper frame tubes, and are retained in position with three mounting bolts. Either tank can be removed and/or installed without disturbing line connections of the other tank.

b. **Fuel Tank.** Fuel tank is located on left side of vehicle and holds slightly over 3 U.S. gallons. It provides mounting for shifter lever and shifter lever guide. Drain is located in forward position on under side of tank.

c. **Oil Tank.** Oil tank is located on right side of vehicle and holds 1 U.S. gallon. Oil feed pipe, scavenger (return) pipe, and breather pipe connections are on under side of tank. Drain is located in forward position on under side of tank.

d. **Remove Fuel Tank.**

(1) Disconnect battery negative ground wire at frame connection.

(2) Loosen the two cap screws which secure caution plate and tank top strip.

(3) Remove instrument panel cover (par. 119).

(4) Disconnect gear shifter lever and shifter rod by removing bolt.

(5) Shut off fuel supply. Disconnect fuel pipe at tank union nipple.

(6) Remove nuts, lock washers, and flat washers from the two front (one upper and one lower) mounting bolts, and nut, lock washer, and flat washer from the rear mounting bolt. Leave bolts in place so that oil tank will stay in position after fuel tank is removed. Remove fuel tank from vehicle.

c. Install Fuel Tank.

(1) Position fuel tank on vehicle. Pass the three mounting bolts through tank brackets from right side of vehicle. It will be necessary to pry up on tank top strip in order to slip top edge of tank under strip. Install large flat washers, lock washers, and nuts on mounting bolts and securely tighten the nuts.

(2) Tighten the two cap screws, securing caution plate and tank top strip.

(3) Connect fuel pipe at tank nipple union. Open supply valve.

(4) Install instrument panel cover (par. 119).

(5) Connect gear shifter lever and shifter rod by installing bolt, lock washer, and nut.

(6) Connect battery negative ground wire to frame connection.

(7) After fuel tank has been filled, check pipe connection and drain plug for leaks.

f. Remove Oil Tank.

(1) Disconnect battery negative ground wire at frame connection.

(2) Loosen the two cap screws which secure caution plate and tank top strip.

(3) Remove instrument panel cover (par. 119).

(4) Drain oil from tank by removing drain plug. Use a trough (of cardboard or tin) to keep oil from draining on engine. NOTE: *If oil feed pipe nipple cap (manufacturer's (H-D) No. 3583-15) is available, it can be screwed on to tank nipple, thus eliminating draining of oil.*

(5) Disconnect oil feed pipe at rear nipple union.

(6) Disconnect scavenger (return) pipe at nipple union.

(7) Disconnect breather pipe banjo-type connection by taking out bolt.

(8) Remove nuts, lock washers, and flat washers from the two front (one upper and one lower) mounting bolts, and nut, lock washer, and flat washer from rear mounting bolt. NOTE: *To prevent fuel tank from falling out of frame, remove upper front mounting bolt and rear mounting bolt and pass both back through fuel tank mounting brackets from the left side of vehicle. Oil tank can then be removed, and fuel tank will stay in place.*

g. Install Oil Tank.

(1) Position oil tank on vehicle. Make sure that composition buffer is in place before installing mounting bolts from right side of vehicle. Pry up on tank top strip in order to slip top edge of tank under strip.

(2) Install large flat washers, lock washers, and nuts on mounting bolts. Securely tighten the nuts.

(3) Tighten the two cap screws securing caution plate and tank top strip.

(4) Connect oil feed pipe to tank nipple. Tank nipple is located at lower rear end of tank.

(5) Connect scavenger (return) pipe to tank nipple. Nipple is located underneath tank, near center.

(6) Connect breather pipe with banjo-type fitting to tank. Use hollow bolt, making sure flat washers are in place on both sides of banjo fitting and that mounting bolt is tight.

(7) Install instrument panel cover (par. 119).

(8) See that oil tank drain plug and washer are in place, and that the plug is tight.

(9) Connect battery negative ground wire to frame connection.

(10) After filling oil tank, check all pipe fittings for leaks.

108. STANDS.

a. Remove Rear Stand. Remove nuts which secure rear stand mounting bolts. Drift bolts out of frame clip holes, freeing stand.

b. Install Rear Stand. Locate stand in position so that bracket stop is downward and will bear against frame axle clips to support vehicle when stand is in use. See that cupped spring washers are on mounting bolts before attaching stand to frame. Drift mounting bolts into frame axle clips and secure with lock washers and nuts.

c. Remove Jiffy Stand.

(1) Support vehicle on rear stand.

(2) Loosen footboard rear support stud nut. Remove footboard front support rod nut and pull footboard outward to release end of safety guard. Remove extended nut from footboard sidebar front mounting. Remove nut securing upper end of skid plate hanger and sidebar rear mounting (located in center of chain guard cover). Loosen nut and bolt which secure skid plate hanger bracket to skid plate; drop bracket. Disconnect clutch control cable from foot pedal stud to prevent damage to cable end piece. Remove left footboard, clutch foot pedal, and sidebar assembly from support rod ends.

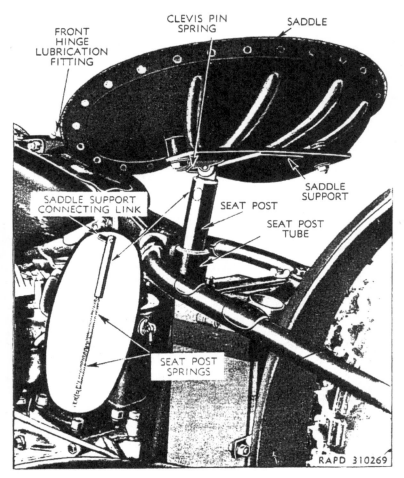

Figure 71—Saddle and Suspension

(3)   Remove the two nuts from U-bolt which secure safety guard bracket to frame tube, remove bracket from U-bolt, and slide safety guard assembly out of support rod.

d. Install Jiffy Stand.

(1) Install safety guard assembly on support rod and secure mounting bracket to frame tube with U-bolt, washers, and nuts.

(2)   Install footboard, clutch foot pedal, and sidebar assembly. Attach skid plate hanger bracket and secure to support rod. Attach

clutch control cable end to foot pedal stud. ; .talling plain washer and cotter pin. Install washer and extended nut on end of front support rod. Securely tighten nut. Attach front end of sidebar to end of safety guard by pulling front of footboard outward, alining hole in safety guard end with hole in sidebar, and passing footboard front support stud through both parts, securing with washer and nut. Tighten footboard rear support stud nut.

(3)   Return vehicle to operating position.

109.   SADDLE POST (fig. 71).

a.   Saddle is mounted on saddle bar by means of three mounting bolts and can be shifted forward or backward to provide three positions on saddle bar. Spacer collars can be added and/or removed from the two rear mountings to raise or lower rear of saddle to alter riding position. Saddle bar hinges on frame bracket and is clevis-connected to saddle spring post. Saddle and saddle bar can be lifted upward and forward after releasing spring latch (on left side) from groove in clevis pin end and removing clevis pin from saddle bar.

b.   **Remove Saddle Spring Post.** Support vehicle on rear stand. Raise saddle and saddle bar after removing saddle post clevis pin. Remove bolt and nut from left-side skid plate bracket and remove nut to free right-side skid plate bracket at muffler pipe clamp and frame connection. Drop skid plate. Remove saddle spring post clamp nut, which is located underneath frame at bottom end of saddle post frame tube. Saddle spring post assembly can be pulled upward out of frame tube.

c.   **Install Saddle Spring Post.** When saddle spring post assembly is inserted in frame tube, see that flat side machined on post rod end nut registers in flat side of hole in bottom of frame tube. Install and securely tighten saddle spring post clamp nut at bottom end of frame tube. Lift skid plate and secure in position with left-side bracket bolt, washer, and nut and with right bracket bolt, washer, and nut (this also secures muffler pipe clamp to frame clip). Lower saddle and saddle bar into position. Insert clevis pin from right side and secure with spring latch, making sure that spring is in pin groove.

110.   SAFETY GUARDS.

a.   **Remove Front Safety Guard.**

(1)   Loosen nuts which secure right and left footboard rear support studs to sidebars. Remove nuts which secure right and left footboard front support studs (and mount ends of safety guard) to sidebars. Pull front end of each footboard outward so that support stud will free end of safety guard. Remove four nuts from the two U-bolts which mount safety guard upper bracket to frame tube. Remove safety guard.

b.   **Install Front Safety Guard.** Locate safety guard and mount upper bracket to frame tube with the two U-bolts, washers, and nuts, but do not tighten nuts as yet. Pull front end of right footboard outward, line up hole in safety guard end with hole in sidebar, and pass footboard front support stud through both parts, securing with washer and nut. Follow same procedure to mount left end of safety guard. Tighten U-bolt nuts securely.

c.   **Remove Rear Safety Guard.** Remove nuts from U-bolts which mount ends of safety guard to lower frame stays. Remove the two nuts from upper safety guard mounting. After removing U-bolts, safety guard can be removed from vehicle.

d.   **Install Rear Safety Guard.** Position safety guard on vehicle. Install U-bolts, washers, and nuts for lower end mounting on frame stays. Do not tighten nuts. Engage upper mounting holes on studs and replace washers and nuts. Tighten all mounting nuts.

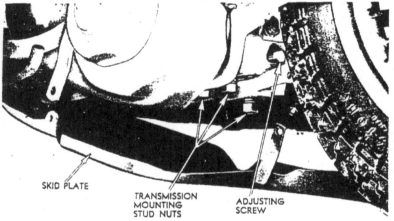

SKID PLATE

TRANSMISSION
MOUNTING
STUD NUTS

ADJUSTING
SCREW

RAPD 310234

Figure 72—Showing Skid Plate Dropped

111.   SKID PLATE.

a.   Rear end of skid plate must be dropped when removing and/or replacing muffler assembly, saddle spring post, transmission, and engine.

b.   **Drop Skid Plate** (fig. 72).

(1)   Remove nut from bolt which secures skid plate side mounting bracket to frame clip. This bolt also mounts muffler tube clamp to frame clip.

(2) Remove left side mounting. Remove nut and bolt which secures lower end of hanger bracket to skid plate on left side of vehicle. Drop rear end of skid plate.

c. Install Dropped Skid Plate.

(1) Lift rear end of skid plate into position. Attach right-side bracket at frame clip bolt. Secure mounting with washer and nut.

(2) Attach lower end of left-side hanger bracket to skid plate. Install bolt. washer, and nut. Tighten nut.

d. Remove and/or Install Skid Plate.

(1) To remove skid plate from vehicle, follow instructions in step b above; then remove nut and bolt from U-clamp which secures skid plate to frame bracket, and remove nut and bolt from clamp which secures right front end to support rod.

(2) To install skid plate, mount right front end to support rod clamp, and install bolt and nut to secure U-clamp under frame bracket. Then follow instructions in step c above.

BATTERY, LIGHTING SYSTEM, HORN

112. DESCRIPTION.

a. Lighting system and horn are supplied 6-volt current from the 22-ampere-hour battery. Negative side of battery and system is grounded. Blackout lights and service lights are controlled by the same switch (ignition and light switch) which also controls ignition. Blackout headlight has auxiliary control switch in body. Service headlight upper and lower beam is controlled by toggle switch on left handle bar. Horn is operated by button on left handle bar after ignition and light switch is in "ON" position. Blackout stop light and service stop light are operated by brake foot pedal switch.

113. BATTERY.

a. The 3-cell, 15-plate, 6-volt, 22-ampere-hour battery is located in battery box back of frame seat post tube, and is accessible for inspection and or service after removing box cover. Normally charged battery has specific gravity reading of 1.275. Normally discharged battery has specific gravity of 1.150.

b. Check Electrolyte Level (fig. 74).

(1) Raise saddle and bar assembly after releasing and removing swivel pin.

(2) Loosen wing thumb nuts on box top hold-down studs sufficiently to disengage bracket slots, then lift off box cover.

(3) Remove the three filler plugs. Check and or adjust electrolyte level. See that electrolyte level is $5/16$ inch above plates. If necessary, bring electrolye to that level, using clean, drinkable water.

(4) Clean top of battery before installing box cover.

(5) Clean terminals or posts, if corroded. Make sure that the felt washers are on posts and are saturated with engine oil.

c. Remove Battery. Raise saddle and bar assembly. Release and remove swivel pin. Loosen wing thumb nuts on box top hold-down studs sufficiently to disengage bracket slots, then lift off box cover.

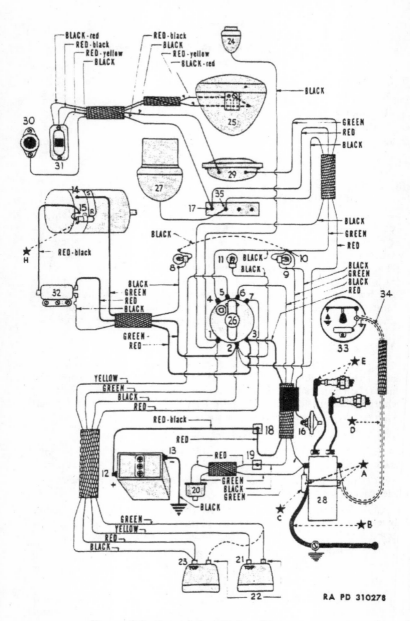

Figure 73—Complete Wiring Diagram

1. SWITCH TERMINAL (Three wires connected)—**Black** wire from blackout marker light 24; taillight cable **green** wire from blackout taillight 22; single wire direct from blackout headlight as shown by dotted line in illustration 43, or horn and headlight cable **black** wire from junction terminal 35 as shown in illustration 44.

2. SWITCH TERMINAL (Four wires connected)—Generator and relay cable **green** wire from **"switch"** terminal (14) of generator; taillight cable **black** wire from service stop and taillight (23); horn and headlight cable **red** wire from junction terminal 17; **black** wire from speedometer light (11).

3. SWITCH TERMINAL (Two wires connected)—Generator and relay cable **red** wire from terminal marked "BAT" on relay; coil and battery cable **red** wire from junction terminal 18.

4. SWITCH TERMINAL (One wire connected)—**Black** wire from oil signal light terminal (10).

5. SWITCH TERMINAL (One wire connected)—Taillight cable **yellow** wire from blackout stop lamp (21).

6. SWITCH TERMINAL (One wire connected)—Battery and coil cable **black** wire from junction terminal 19.

7. SWITCH TERMINAL (One wire connected)—Taillight cable **red** wire from service stop and taillight (23).

8. GENERATOR SIGNAL LIGHT TERMINAL (One wire connected)—Generator and relay cable **black** wire from relay right front terminal.

9. OIL PRESSURE SIGNAL LIGHT TERMINAL (One wire connected)—**Black** wire from oil pressure switch (16).

10. SIGNAL LIGHT TERMINAL (Four wires connected)—**Black** wire (under switch panel) from generator signal light terminal (8); **black** wire from switch terminal (4); battery and coil cable **green** wire from coil front terminal; horn and headlight cable **green** wire from horn.

11. SPEEDOMETER LIGHT—**Black** wire from switch terminal 2.

12. BATTERY POSITIVE TERMINAL (LEFT SIDE)—**Red** wire with **black tracer** from junction terminal 18.

13. BATTERY NEGATIVE TERMINAL (RIGHT SIDE)—**Black** wire from ground clamp on frame.

14. "SWITCH" TERMINAL OF GENERATOR—Generator and relay cable **green** wire from switch terminal 2.

15. "RELAY" TERMINAL OF GENERATOR—**Red** wire with **black tracer** from relay rear terminal.

16. OIL PRESSURE SIGNAL SWITCH—**Black** wire from signal light terminal 9.

17. JUNCTION TERMINAL (BAKELITE TERMINAL PLATE ON HORN MOUNTING)—Horn and headlight cable **red** wire from switch terminal 2; **red** wire with **black tracer** from handlebar toggle switch (31).

18. FRONT JUNCTION TERMINAL (in motorcycle frame, under saddle)—Coil and battery cable **red** wire from switch terminal 3; **red** wire with **black tracer** from battery positive terminal (12).

19. REAR JUNCTION TERMINAL (in motorcycle frame, under saddle)—Coil and battery cable **black** wire from switch terminal 6; **red** wire from stop light switch (20).

RA PD 310278B

Legend for Figure 73—Complete Wiring Diagram

20. STOP LIGHT SWITCH—**Red** wire from junction terminal 19; **green** wire from coil terminal.

21. BLACKOUT STOP LIGHT (Top socket in right taillight)—Taillight cable **yellow** wire from switch terminal 5.

22. BLACKOUT TAILLIGHTS—Taillight cable **green** wire from switch terminal 1.

23. SERVICE TAIL AND STOP LIGHT (top socket in left taillight —two wires in one plug)—Taillight cable **black** wire from switch terminal 2 is for service taillight, and taillight cable **red** wire from switch terminal 7 is for service stop light.

24. BLACKOUT MARKER LIGHT (ON FRONT MUDGUARD)— **Black** wire from switch terminal 1.

25. SERVICE HEADLIGHT—**Black** wire with **red tracer** from handlebar toggle switch (31) to large terminal screw; **red** wire with **yellow tracer** from handlebar toggle switch to small terminal screw.

26. IGNITION AND LIGHT SWITCH (TOP VIEW)—Switch "OFF" in straight-ahead position.

27. BLACKOUT HEADLIGHT— Blackout headlight is fitted with independent switch in lamp body.

28. SPARK COIL—Coil and battery cable **green** wire from terminal 10 to coil front terminal; **green** wire from stop light switch (20) to coil front terminal; low tension wire (34) from circuit breaker (33) to coil rear terminal.

29. HORN—Horn and headlight cable **green** wire from terminal 10; **black** wire from horn switch (30).

☆ 30. HORN SWITCH—**Black** wire from horn.

31. HANDLEBAR TOGGLE SWITCH —**Black** wire with **red tracer** from service headlight terminal with large terminal screw; **red** wire with **yellow tracer** to service headlight terminal with small terminal screw; **red** wire with **black tracer** from junction terminal 17.

32. CUT-OUT RELAY—**Red** wire with **black tracer** from "relay" terminal of generator to relay rear terminal; generator and relay cable **red** wire from switch terminal 3 to relay terminal marked "BAT"; generator and relay cable **black** wire from terminal 8, to relay right front terminal.

33. IGNITION CIRCUIT BREAKER AND TIMER—Low tension wire (34) from coil rear terminal.

34. CIRCUIT BREAKER-TO-COIL LOW TENSION WIRE—See Description 33.

35. JUNCTION TERMINAL ON BAKELITE TERMINAL PLATE— Horn and headlight cable **black** wire from switch terminal 1; wire from blackout headlight (27).

All WLA model motorcycles originally equipped with radio interference suppression-devices, or to which suppression-devices have been added, can be identified by a large letter S stenciled on left and right sides of instrument panel cover.

★**A** GROUND TERMINALS ON COIL HOUSING.

★**B** FLEXIBLE BRAID CONDUCTOR.

★**C** CONDENSER.

★**D** SHIELDED CIRCUIT BREAKER-TO-COIL LOW TENSION WIRE.

★**E** SPARK PLUG SUPPRESSORS.

★**H** CONDENSER.   RA PD 310278C

☆

Legend for Figure 73—Complete Wiring Diagram

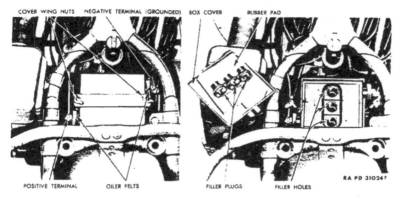

Figure 74—Battery Box Open and Filler Plugs Removed for Service

Disconnect positive and negative wires from battery terminals. Lift battery upward out of battery box.

d.   **Install Battery.** See that rubber mat is in place in bottom of battery box and install battery in box so that positive post is on left side of vehicle, and negative post is on right side of vehicle. Connect wires to battery positive and negative posts. Fit rubber mat on top of battery. Install cover and securely tighten thumb wing nuts. Lower saddle and bar assembly. Install swivel pin on right side of vehicle so that retaining spring fits in groove in end of swivel pin.

114.   HEADLIGHTS.

a.   **Service Headlight.**

(1)   Remove nut which secures light body to bracket, observing that conical washer bears against cup of bracket for secure light mounting. Disconnect wires from light body terminals.

(2)   Before installing service headlight, connect wires to light body terminals, noting that black wire with red tracer connects with the larger terminal screw. Mount light on bracket. Position conical-shaped washer and lock washer and install mounting stud nut. Do not tighten mounting nut.

b.   **Adjust Service Headlight.** Adjustment should be made in darkened area or at night, tactical situation permitting. Vehicle must be standing on a level surface about 25 feet away from and headed toward a wall or screen upon which a horizontal line has been drawn at exactly the same height as service headlight center. Set handle bar toggle switch in "BRIGHT" position and check light beam for height and direction. The top of main beam of light should register on wall or screen even with, but not higher than, the horizontal line mentioned. Tilt light body in bracket up or down to correctly aim it in relation to the horizontal line, making sure that

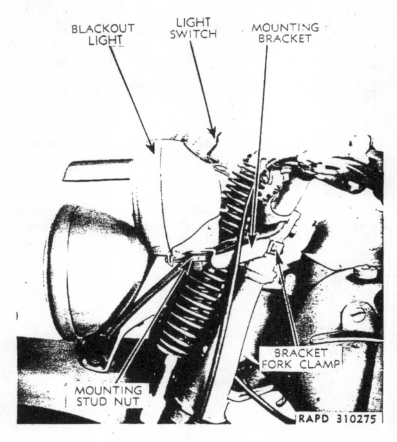

Figure 75—Blackout Headlight Installation

light body is not turned either to right or left. Securely tighten mounting stud nut.

c.   **Blackout Headlight.** Blackout headlight is mounted on bracket which attaches to left upper side of front fork. Blackout headlight operates when ignition and light switch is turned to the second right position. However, blackout headlight is fitted with an independent switch in light body to permit turning it off while other blackout lights are in use. Blackout headlight body is secured to mounting bracket by means of a conical washer, lock washer, and mounting nut, providing a swivel mounting to permit light adjustment.

d. **Blackout Marker Light.** The blackout marker light is secured to front mudguard by means of a hollow mounting stud, with plain washer, lock washer, and nut. Light wire passes through hollow stud and is protected by tubing on under side of mudguard. Blackout marker light wire connects with No. 1 post on ignition and light switch. Lamp is on with ignition and light switch in second right position.

115. TAILLIGHTS.

a. **Blackout Stop and Taillight.** Blackout stop and taillight is mounted on right side of taillight bracket. Light is provided with top unit to provide blackout stop light controlled by brake-operated

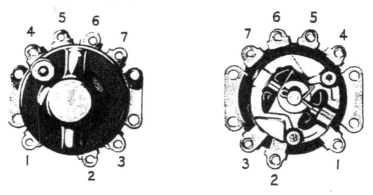

RAPD 310272

Figure 76—Ignition and Light Switch, Front and Back Positions

stop light switch. Bottom unit in the blackout stop and taillight is regularly used as service blackout taillight and is controlled by ignition and light switch.

b. **Service Stop and Taillight.** Light is located on left side of light mounting bracket. Top unit is used for service stop and taillight (double filament lamp). Taillight filament is controlled by ignition and light switch; stop lamp filament is controlled by brake-operated stop light switch. Stop light does not operate in daytime when ignition only is turned on. Bottom unit serves as a spare blackout taillight. In case the regularly used (right-side) blackout taillamp fails, its socket plug can be transferred to this taillight socket.

c. **Stop and Taillight Switch.** This switch is operated by brake pedal and is located on end of rear support rod on right side of vehicle. Refer to wiring diagram (fig. 73) and paragraph 118 for wiring connections.

116. IGNITION AND LIGHT SWITCH.

a. Earlier models are provided with lock, later models are non-locking.

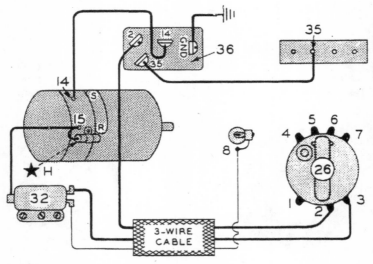

8—GENERATOR SIGNAL LIGHT.
14—GENERATOR TERMINAL TO SWITCH.
15—GENERATOR TERMINAL TO RELAY.
26—IGNITION-LIGHT SWITCH.
32—RELAY
35—TERMINAL STRIP BINDING POST.
36—MAGNETIC SWITCH FOR BLACKOUT LIGHT.
H—NOISE SUPPRESSION CONDENSER.

RAPD 310279

Figure 77—Blackout Headlight Magnetic Switch on Later Models

b. **Remove.** Disconnect battery ground wire. Remove instrument panel cover (par. 119). Disconnect all wires from switch. Remove the four switch mounting screws and spacers. Switch is now free for removal.

c. **Install.** Mount switch on instrument panel base. Install four screws and spacers. Connect wires (fig. 73). Connect battery negative ground wire to frame. Turn switch on. Check lights and horn, tactical situation permitting. Install instrument panel cover (par. 119).

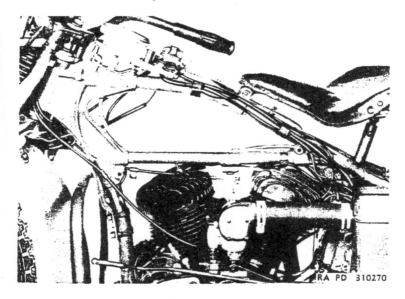

Figure 78—Wiring Cables, Left Side

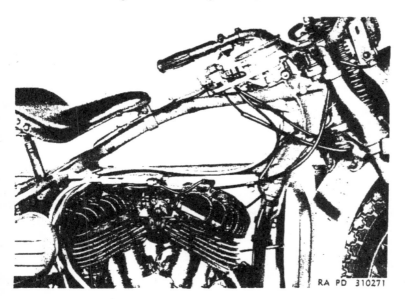

Figure 79—Wiring Cables, Right Side

117. HORN.

a. **Description.** Horn is mounted to headlight bracket by means of four bolts, lock washers, and nuts. One horn terminal is connected with operating button, and other terminal is connected to No. 4 ignition and light switch terminal (fig. 73).

b. **Adjust.** Tone adjusting screw is located in rear side of horn. If horn fails to operate and moving the adjusting screw does not remedy the trouble, horn must be replaced. NOTE: *Do not change position of the adjusting screw located in center of diaphragm.*

118. WIRING.

a. **Cable System.** Since ignition and lights are controlled by the ignition and light switch, all wires terminate at the ignition and light switch. Cables for wire protection are used, making it necessary to replace cables rather than individual wires. A study of figure 73 will be helpful when removing or installing any of the wiring cables. Also study figures 78 and 79 and note how cables are arranged on frame, and how they lead to the switch panel.

b. **Remove and Install Cables.** When it becomes necessary to replace wiring cables leading to the ignition and light switch, both fuel and oil tanks must be removed (par. 107) and instrument panel cover removed (par. 119) for accessibility.

INSTRUMENT PANEL

119. PANEL COVER (fig. 80).

a. **Remove.** Remove speedometer light switch knob and remove screw. Remove hexagon-head screw on front of cover. Remove two screws from side of cover. Remove two screws and washers which fasten plate to right side of cover. Lift cover off panel.

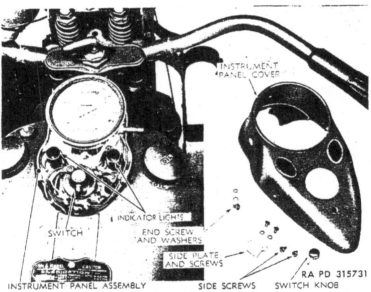

Figure 80—Panel Cover Removed

b. **Install.** Position cover on panel. Install two side mounting screws and washers and install hexagon-head screw. plain washer. and lock washer in front end of cover. Attach cover side plate. installing two screws and washers. Install speedometer light switch knob and screw.

120. INDICATOR LIGHTS.

a. Three 2-c.p. single-contact lamps are located on instrument panel. One for oil pressure (red) indicator light: one for generator-charge (green) indicator light, and one for speedometer illumination.

b. **Remove and/or Install.** Remove and/or install panel cover (par. 119).

c. **Test Generator-Charge (Green) Indicator Lamp.** Disconnect black wire from relay terminal (top terminal at front end of relay) and ground on relay base. Turn ignition and light switch on. Lamp should light. If it does not light, check wire for condition and/or replace lamp after removing panel cover (par. 119).

d. **Test Oil Pressure (Red) Indicator Lamp.** Disconnect wire from oil pressure switch. Ground the wire on engine. Turn ignition and light switch on. Lamp should light. If it does not light, check wire for condition and/or replace lamp after removing panel cover (par. 119). If lamp and wiring are satisfactory, replace oil pressure switch.

121. SPEEDOMETER HEAD.

a. **Remove.** Remove instrument panel cover (par. 119). Loosen the two tank front mounting bolts and remove rear mounting bolt to free speedometer cable clamp. Disconnect speedometer cable at drive unit. Free cable from clip located below tool box. Remove two screws which mount head to frame. Pull head upward, working cable forward under tank, until head and cable connection nut is clear of frame. Unscrew cable nut. NOTE: *Cable may be secured to frame tube, between tanks, with friction tape. If so, cut tape.*

b. **Install.** Attach speedometer head to cable end and tighten nut. Pass cable down into frame hole, pulling on rear of cable at same time. Mount speedometer head to frame with two screws and lock washers. Install panel cover (par. 119). Secure cable clamp under head of tank rear mounting bolt. Secure cable in clip, located under tool box. Attach end of cable to drive unit. Tighten the two tank front mounting bolts.

TIRES, WHEELS, AND HUBS

122. DESCRIPTION.

a. Wheels have drop center rims to accommodate 4.00 x 18 tires. Front and rear wheels are not interchangeable. Front wheel hub is of ball-bearing design, having cone adjustment similar to that of a bicycle hub. Rear wheel hub is of roller-bearing design and must be taken apart for adjustment. Both wheels have "knock-out" type axles.

123. TIRES.

a. **Description.** Wheel rims are of the drop-center type, having a depression, or well, in center of rim. The rim well, being smaller in circumference than the rest of the rim, allows one casing bead to fit loosely in it while other bead is being worked over edge of rim. Bear in mind the importance of keeping one bead in rim well while other bead is being worked onto or off rim. NOTE: *It is not always necessary to completely remove casing from rim. Removing one side only allows inner tube to be removed and reinstalled, and also allows inside of casing to be inspected.*

b. **Remove.**

(1) Remove wheel from vehicle and lay wheel on its side. To remove front wheel, refer to paragraph 125. To remove rear wheel, refer to paragraph 127.

(2) Remove valve cap and valve core to free all air from tube.

(3) Press casing head into rim well to within a short distance of each side of valve.

(4) Using tire iron "B" in vehicle kit (fig. 11), start bead over edge of rim at valve. Do not use force when starting bead over edge of rim with tire iron, because bead wires may be broken or stretched, and tire ruined. With first bead in rim well, bead on other side can be started easily over edge of rim. After a portion of second bead is started over rim edge, casing can be further removed from wheel without aid of tire iron.

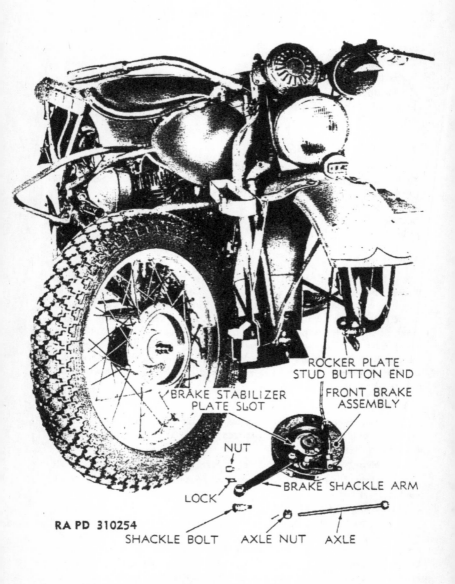

ROCKER PLATE
STUD BUTTON END

FRONT BRAKE
ASSEMBLY

BRAKE STABILIZER
PLATE SLOT

NUT

BRAKE SHACKLE ARM

LOCK

RA PD 310254

SHACKLE BOLT   AXLE NUT   AXLE

Figure 81—Disassembly for Front Wheel Removal

c. **Install.** Before applying casing to rim, see that rubber rim strip is in place in rim well and that rim strip valve hole alines with valve hole in rim.

(1) Start either bead of casing over rim edge. Work around wheel until entire bead is on rim.

(2) Place inner tube in casing. NOTE: *Inner tube may be placed in casing before or after first bead of casing is on rim.* Insert valve stem through hole in rim and start valve stem lock nut. While pressing first bead into rim well, work remaining bead over edge of rim, starting directly opposite valve stem. Work both ways around wheel toward valve.

(3) Inflate front tire to 18 pounds, and rear tire to 20 pounds.

(4) Reinstall front wheel (par. 125); reinstall wheel (par. 127). CAUTION: *Tire casings are balanced and must be applied to rim with balance mark located at valve stem. On Firestone tires the balance mark is a red triangle, and on Goodyear tires a red dot.*

124. RIMS AND SPOKES.

a. Wheels with broken and/or missing spokes, with rims in badly kinked and/or distorted condition, or having considerable run-out, must be replaced.

b. Loose wheel spokes must be tightened evenly, being careful not to distort rim out-of-round or cause run-out. Use spoke nipple wrench (41-W-3339) for front wheel spokes, and wrench (41-W-3340) for rear wheel spokes.

125. FRONT WHEEL REPLACEMENT (fig. 81).

a. **Remove.**

(1) Support vehicle on rear stand. Raise front end of vehicle by blocking up under frame loop on skid plate.

(2) Remove brake shackle bolt from rigid fork on left side of vehicle.

(3) Front axle is knock-out type. Remove cotter pin and axle castle nut and pull out axle. Wheel is free for removal. CAUTION: *Before removing axle note how slot in brake stabilizer plate is fitted over the extended (button) end of the left-front rocker plate stud. It is necessary that this be correctly assembled when replacing front wheel.*

(4) Roll wheel forward and remove brake assembly from brake drum, leaving the assembly attached to brake control wire and control wire housing.

b. Install (fig. 81). NOTE: *At the time wheel and brake assembly is located in front fork, and before axle is installed, make sure that the curved slot in brake stabilizer plate engages with the button end of the left-front rocker plate stud.*

(1) Install brake assembly in brake drum.

(2) Roll wheel into position. Engage stabilizer plate notch and rocker plate stud button end, and at same time insert front axle.

(3) Install castle nut (no lock washer used) on axle and securely tighten.

Figure 82—Front Hub Prepared for Cone Adjustment

(4) Use good cotter pin to secure nut.

(5) Install brake shackle bolt and special lock washer and nut. Tighten nut.

(6) Check front brake control wire and housing to make sure everything is in order and correctly adjusted (par. 97).

(7) Remove blocking from under vehicle.

126. FRONT WHEEL HUB ADJUSTMENT.

a. Front wheel, ball-bearing hub. is similar to a bicycle front hub as far as adjustment is concerned. Do not completely disassemble hub for adjustment as balls are not in retainers. and will fall out when cone is removed. Hub is provided with grease deflector sleeve and felt retainer. NOTE: *Earlier models are not equipped with grease deflector sleeve or felt retainer washer. Front wheel should have slight play or shake on bearings, and should turn freely.*

Figure 83—Disassembly for Rear Wheel Removal

(1) Remove front wheel (par. 125).

(2) Back off cone lock nut to end of axle sleeve. Do not remove nut.

(3) Turn cone on axle sleeve to the right (clockwise) to take up wheel play, and to the left (counterclockwise) to give more wheel play. Adjust so that wheel has slight play on bearing.

(4) Tighten cone lock nut. After tightening nut, again try for slight wheel play on bearing. Sometimes tightening lock nut takes up on bearing play. If necessary, readjust for desired results when cone lock nut is tight.

(5) Install front wheel and brake assembly (par. 125).

(6) Check adjustment of front brake.

127. REAR WHEEL REPLACEMENT (figs. 83 and 84).

a. Remove.

(1) Support vehicle on rear stand.

(2) Release mudguard rear stays. Loosen mounting nuts, and raise end of mudguard for wheel clearance.

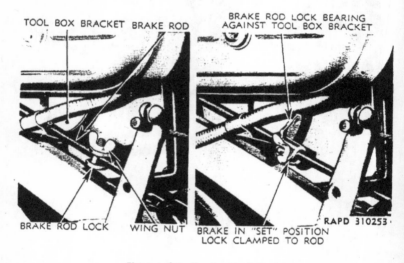

Figure 84—Brake Rod Lock

(3) Remove the five wheel mounting socket screws which secure wheel hub to brake shell and sprocket assembly. Use vehicle kit wrench "S" and sleeve (handle) "C" (fig. 11). NOTE: *Wrench can be inserted from left side through holes in hub, and wheel must be turned to bring each mounting screw directly to the rear of axle for accessibility.*

(4) Use brake rod lock to set and lock brake to prevent brake shell and sprocket from coming off brake assembly while wheel is being removed. Apply brake pedal and shift brake rod lock against

tool box bracket, securing lock in this position with wing nut (fig. 84).

(5) Remove axle nut (right side of vehicle), using vehicle kit wrench "J" (fig. 11).

(6) Pull out axle from left side of vehicle.

(7) Remove spacer from between wheel hub end and left side of frame.

(8) Wheel is now free to come out by pulling and working it away from dowel pins located in brake shell assembly. A wheel being removed for the first time may offer some resistance. It will be observed that chain, sprocket, and brake assembly remain in the vehicle frame.

b. **Install** (figs. 83 and 84).

(1) Position wheel on brake shell dowel pins. Work hub onto dowels as far as it will go.

(2) Install axle spacer at left end of hub so that axle will pass through it and the hub.

(3) Install axle from left side of vehicle. Pass it through sleeve and hub, with end of axle engaging the frame left axle clip notch.

(4) See that lock washer is in place. Turn on and securely tighten axle nut, using vehicle kit wrench "J" (fig. 11).

(5) Loosen wing nut clamping brake rod lock. Move brake rod lock forward so that it will not strike any object when brake is operated; tighten wing nut to retain in position (fig. 84).

(6) Install and securely tighten the five wheel mounting socket screws.

(7) Lower mudguard into position and attach ends of rear stays. Securely tighten the clamping nuts.

REFERENCES

STANDARD NOMENCLATURE LISTS

Motorcycle, chain drive (Harley-Davidson)	SNL G-523
Cleaning, preserving and lubricating materials, recoil fluids, special oils, and miscellaneous related items	SNL K-1
Soldering, brazing, and welding materials, gases, and related items	SNL K-2
Tools, maintenance, for the repair of automotive vehicles	SNL G-27
Tool sets—motor transport	SNL N-19
Tool sets for ordnance service command, automotive shops	SNL N-30
Current Standard Nomenclature Lists are listed above.	
An up-to-date list of SNL's is maintained in the Index to Maintenance Publications	OFSB 1-1

EXPLANATORY PUBLICATIONS

Military motor vehicles	AR 850-15

Automotive Materiel

Automotive electricity	TM 10-580
Electric fundamentals	TM 10-455
The motor vehicle	TM 10-510
Chassis, body, and trailer units	TM 10-550

Maintenance and Repair

Automotive lubrication	TM 10-540
Motor transport inspections	TM 10-545
Tire repair and retread	TM 9-1868
Cleaning, preserving, lubricating and welding materials and similar items issued by the ordnance	TM 9-850
Detailed lubrication instructions for ordnance materiel	OFSB 6-series

Protection of Materiel

Explosives and demolitions	FM 5-25
Defense against chemical attack	FM 21-40
Decontamination of Armored Force vehicles	FM 17-59
Chemical decontamination, materials and equipment	TM 3-220

List of Publications for Training

	FM 21-6

Storage and Shipment

Registration of motor vehicles	AR 850-10
Storage of motor vehicle equipment	AR 850-18
Ordnance storage and shipment chart, group G— Major items	OSSC-G

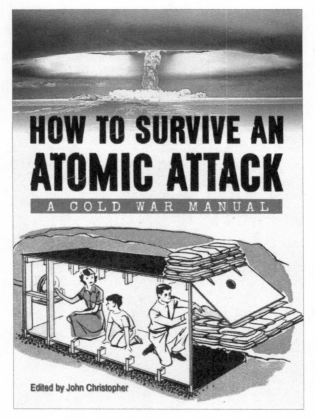

The Great War Cook Book
May Byron

With over 500 wartime recipes, May Byron offers unusual
alternatives to traditional ingredients in a Britain almost starved into
submission.

978 1 4456 3388 6
231 pages

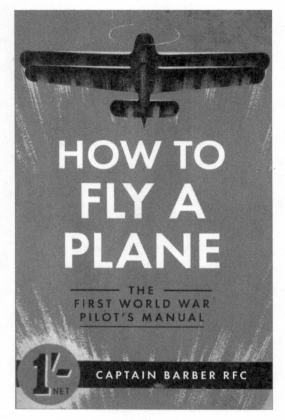

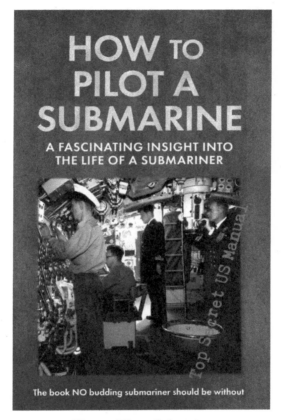

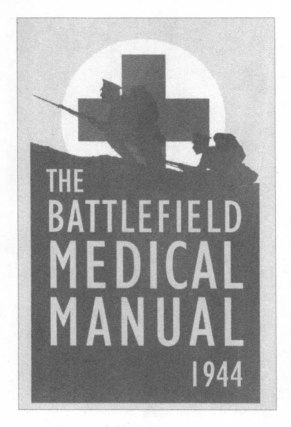

How to Drive a Car

Motor Magazine

A fascinating insight into driving in the 1920s and 1930s.

978 1 4456 3579 8
160 pages

ALSO AVAILABLE FROM AMBERLEY PUBLISHING

Hurricane Manual 1940
Dilip Sarker

The Hawker Hurricane was a vital stalwart of the British war effort.
Here, for the first time, Dilip Sarker collates all the training anuals and
notes on how to fly a Hurricane.

978 1 4456 2120 3
256 pages

Available from all good bookshops or order direct
from our website www.amberley-books.com

Spitfire Manual 1940
Dilip Sarker

How to fly the legendary fighter plane in combat using the manuals
and instructions supplied by the RAF during the Second World War.

978 1 84868 436 2
288 pages

Available from all good bookshops or order direct
from our website www.amberley-books.com

Land Girl Manual 1941
W. E. Shewell-Cooper

A fabulous piece of wartime nostalgia, a facsimile edition of the
manual used by the Land Girls during the Second World War.

978 1 4456 0279 0
160 pages

ALSO AVAILABLE FROM AMBERLEY PUBLISHING

Train Driver's Manual
Colin Maggs

Colin Maggs has assembled a fascinating collection of illustrated
railwayman's handbooks. You want to be a train driver? This book
answers all your questions.

978 1 4456 1680 3
304 pages

Available from all good bookshops or order direct
from our website www.amberley-books.com

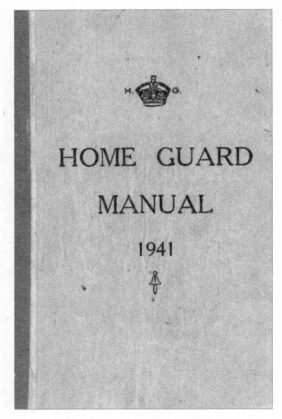